"There is purpose and meaning for our ⬛⬛⬛ in a way that honors our Lord and Savic ⬛⬛⬛ rich understanding of this subject. This book is a must-read."

C. William Pollard, chairman emeritus
The ServiceMaster Company

"My own kingdom zeal has been renewed by this compelling 'little' book. Built off the life-changing truths of the Wesleyan tradition—which are, themselves, so solidly built on the living Word of God—this timely read is for anyone who desires their work to express the transforming character of Christ. And in so doing, change their co-workers. Their communities. Their world."

Harold Smith, president and CEO
Christianity Today

"As David Wright and his team point out, most of us spend the greatest portion of our waking hours doing our work, whether it's in a paying job or in the other forms work can take. What then could be more important than working in such a way that we are enriched by our endeavors and we also contribute to the well-being of our communities and ultimately our world? *How God Makes the World a Better Place* distills principles drawn from Scripture, and from the lives and works of John and Charles Wesley, that help us live into both what God has called us to be as followers of Jesus Christ and what he has uniquely called each of us to do."

David "Mac" McQuiston, president and CEO
CEO Forum, Inc.

"David Wright and his team have done a marvelous job of compiling many insights from the writings of John Wesley in this book. At a time in history when work and accomplishments are being battered by some, it is good to see a book written about the positive and spiritual aspects of work. John Wesley had a healthy definition of work as is shown throughout this book. The book shows the connection between our spiritual lives and our work lives. *There should be no distance between them.* Enjoy this refreshing book of advice and testimonials about the blessings of working as unto the Lord."

Barbara Green, cofounder, Hobby Lobby

"It is a privilege for me to offer an endorsement of *How God Makes the World a Better Place.* First of all, as I have gotten to know Dr. Wright, I see true authenticity in every area of his life and work. Secondly, the message is sorely needed in this very confused world. My work really does matter, not only today, but for all of eternity, and that point is well made. Thirdly, this book is very well written and readable. The stories make a point and are compelling. No matter how old or young you are in the faith or how you spend your working hours, this book will minister greatly to you."

Ron Blue, president, Kingdom Advisors
The Ron Blue Institute for Financial Planning
Indiana Wesleyan University

HOW GOD
MAKES THE WORLD
A BETTER PLACE

Primers in This Series

HOW GOD
MAKES THE WORLD
A BETTER PLACE

A Wesleyan Primer on Faith, Work,
and Economic Transformation

DAVID WRIGHT

with contributions by
Rebecca Whitesel, Christin Taylor,
Patrick Eby, and Keith Reeves

With a Foreword by
Jo Anne Lyon

Christian's LIBRARY PRESS

GRAND RAPIDS · MICHIGAN

Unless otherwise indicated, all Scripture quotations are from the Holy Bible, NEW INTERNATIONAL VERSION®. Copyright © 1973, 1978, 1984 by Biblica, Inc. All rights reserved worldwide. Used by permission.

Permission from the copyright holders to quote from the following sources is gratefully acknowledged:

Excerpts from interview by Christin Taylor with Katei Kirby (part 1), used by permission.

Excerpts from interviews by Rebecca Whitesel with Wilbur Williams (part 3, chap. 1), Ralph Hodges (part 3, chap. 2), Chris Foley (part 3, chap. 3), Jenny (part 4, chap. 4), George and Esther Jetter (part 4, chap. 4), Keith Stanton (part 4, chap. 5), Tom and Joan Phillippe (part 4, chap. 6), Ken Sloane (part 4, chap. 6), and Tom Collins (conclusion), used by permission.

In some cases, personal names in vignettes or stories have been changed to protect privacy.

Excerpts from online text of various sermons by John Wesley (part 3; part 3, chap. 2; part 4; part 4, chap. 4; part 4, chap. 6) and of a letter from John Wesley to Miss March (part 4, chap. 5), the Wesley Center for Applied Theology, Northwest Nazarene University, wesley.nnu.edu.

Excerpts from "The History of Boots the Chemist—Nottingham," (part 4, chap. 4), used by permission of NgTrader, ngtrader.co.uk/thebootsstory.htm.

Excerpts from "Religion" (part 4, chap. 5), used by permission of Cornish Mining World Heritage, www.cornish-mining.org.uk/delving-deeper/religion, © Cornwall Council, reproduction by permission."

Excerpts from online text of John Wesley, *The Character of a Methodist* (part 4, chap. 6), used by permission of Global Ministries, www.umcmission.org.

ISBN 978-1-938948-17-6 (paperback)

Christian's Library Press
An imprint of the Acton Institute for the Study of Religion & Liberty
161 Ottawa Ave. NW, Suite 301
Grand Rapids, Michigan 49503
www.clpress.com

Cover and interior design by Sharon VanLoozenoord
Editing by Stephen J. Grabill, Timothy J. Beals, and Paul J. Brinkerhoff

21 20 19 18 17 16 15 14 13 12   1 2 3 4 5 6 7 8 9 10
Printed in the United States of America
First edition

Contents

Foreword

The common question "What kind of work do you do?" is the typical conversation starter at many social events. Depending on the curiosity of the participants, the discussion can have many facets and much can be learned. However, rarely does this lead to the deeper meaning of "work."

Almost daily we are reminded of the massive unemployment throughout the world. A nation's gross domestic product is very dependent on employment. The linkages of crime and unemployment haunt us daily. But again, how does this connect with discipleship and making the world a better place?

A theme I regularly hear is "I really want to do something meaningful," or "I want to change jobs and do something that gives me satisfaction." Essentially I have heard a similar theme from the poorest of the poor. "I don't want to just have you give me something; I want to work." Deep in the human heart is the desire to have one's work "make a difference." Perhaps it is as Dorothy L. Sayers has argued, that "work is the natural exercise and function of humans—the creature who is made in the image of his or her Creator." ("Why Work?" in *Creed or Chaos?*) John Paul II takes it even a step further in *Laborem Exercens* and talks about work as humans sharing in the image of their Creator. This primer follows the same theme. The life stories reach around the world and through the economic spectrum and yet come out at the same place . . . work as cooperation with God.

This is not about a glamorous career or finally finding the "right job." This is about every person's daily life lived to the full no matter the work or location. This primer explores John Wesley's

teaching, particularly of work, in very practical terms. To put succinctly what this book is about, David Wright says it well in chapter 6, that "in the Wesleyan view, godly work is not defined by
what one does, but by the way one does it."

Perhaps even more compelling in this primer are the pen-
etrating discussion questions following the life stories and how
these questions are integrated with Wesley's teachings. I must ad-
mit that in writing this foreword I have been delayed by my own
internal dialogue wrestling with some of the concepts.

Chapter 4, "Work That Promotes Personal Well-Being," could
be interpreted in our current culture as "all about me." But it is exactly the opposite. Here in this chapter one discovers that the view
of the eighteenth century literally turns the twenty-first century
on its head and sees the world from another perspective. There
David Wright writes, "[John and Charles Wesley] called Wesleyans to embrace both the beauty and the ugliness of the world. The
people of the Wesleyan movement were called to engage with both
the opportunities and the brokenness they saw around them.
They could neither ignore, nor accept as inevitable, the hurt and
brokenness in their world." What a contrast to our current culture of pursuing our own happiness at the expense of others. The
Wesleyan call is about our work of restoring the world in the image of God.

Perhaps some of the old hymns regarding work had this
premise in mind. Somehow as I reflected on them I saw them in
new light, such as Fanny Crosby's "To the Work":

> To the Work, To the Work! We are servants of God,
> Let us follow the path that our Master has trod;
> With the might of His power our strength to renew,
> Let us do by His grace what He calls us to do.

Or Anna Coghill's "Work, for the Night is Coming":

Work, for the night is coming,
Work through the morning hours;
Work while the dew is sparkling,
Work 'mid springing flowers;
Work when the day grows brighter,
Work in the glowing sun;
Work, for the night is coming,
When man's work is done.

Or Elizabeth Mills's "We'll Work Till Jesus Comes":

We'll work till Jesus comes
We'll work till Jesus comes
We'll work till Jesus comes
And we'll be gathered home.

What would happen if all readers of *How God Makes the World a Better Place* would read it in community and begin practicing the principles with accountability? Could we imagine the world as a better place? Could we imagine people influencing their workplace with new hope and vision? Could we imagine people seeing everything they are doing as "making a difference"? We have the example of the eighteenth-century Wesleyan revivals. It is not beyond our imagination! Perhaps God even wants to do more and do a "*new* thing" in the twenty-first century. Even this primer could be a catalyst for such a move!

Jo Anne Lyon
general superintendent
The Wesleyan Church

Introduction

This little book is dedicated to one purpose. Our aim is to help you make your work and the work of your fellow employees a lifelong source of well-being and fulfillment. We believe the key to this achievement is to learn how to be fully devoted followers of Jesus at work.

Why is this important?

Work is one of life's most important pursuits. It can be drudgery and a curse or it can also be one of life's most powerful sources of personal and community blessing. It is important for followers of Jesus Christ to know how to make their life's work a source of well-being for at least four reasons:

First, you will probably spend more time doing your work than any other single activity in your waking life. Doesn't it make sense to get right the one thing you will spend most of your time and energy doing?

Second, your life's material resources will come from your work. If you work with purpose and wisdom throughout your life, you will reap material rewards. If you work aimlessly, you will struggle to manage the stream of resources that God will send through your hands.

Third, your work is the primary way you will bless others. If you are fortunate, you will be able to give generously to others throughout your life. But no matter how generous you are, for all but a very few of the greatest philanthropists, the fruit of our work will be the greatest blessing we give to others. When we work, we take part in the social network of the economy, creating goods and services of value to others. If you work selfishly, you will impoverish those around you, and ultimately you will destroy yourself. If you work with a heart to serve, you will enrich those around you, and you will bring stability and well-being into your own life and the lives of others.

Fourth, few things in life generate a sense of well-being, or conversely, erode well-being, as powerfully as your work. Whether it is in the form of a recognized career—a "paying job"—or in one of the many other forms, your work will be a central contribution to your sense of self-esteem, your identity, and your overall well-being and the well-being of others. Further, when good work is available, visible, and rewarded in our communities, all of us gain a sense of self-esteem, identity, and well-being.

Two Distinctions

Now, let's make a couple of distinctions.

First, there is a difference between your work and your job. Specific jobs will come and go throughout your life. Very few of us will have the same employer throughout our working lives. Jobs are important. We must value them and do them well. But jobs are healthiest when they are viewed as expressions of the work to which each of us has been called. Ultimately, our self-esteem, prosperity, and well-being come from our work. Our jobs are the places we invest our work.

Another distinction we should make early on in this study is that this isn't a book about managing money. Money and work are surely linked. The link between work and money is one of the most beautiful concepts of God's creation. But we don't have time in this little primer to review the principles of wise management of the money that your work will produce. For that wisdom we recommend our good friend and colleague Ron Blue and the Ron Blue Institute for Financial Planning. No one is better than Ron at teaching biblical principles for managing our money. In this book we will stick to talking about the pursuit that will produce most of the money we will have to manage throughout our lives—our work.

Principles from a Wesleyan Heritage

We approach this topic as members of the family of approximately 70 million Christians worldwide whose spiritual heritage comes from the ministry of John and Charles Wesley. We are writing explicitly for those whose faith has been shaped in the Wesleyan tradition. Nevertheless, we gladly offer these principles of whole-life discipleship to the whole body of Jesus' followers. We write this book for anyone who wants to understand the great truths about the way God designed work, service, and economic transformation to function in this world.

John and Charles Wesley were passionately devoted to their calling as Christian ministers. A part of this calling was to make their English homeland a better place. They lived in one of the most challenging periods of England's history, the dawn of the Industrial Revolution in England. Their work, blessed by God's presence, transformed millions of lives and changed England for the better religiously, socially, and economically.

What allowed John and Charles to have such a great impact? The central emphasis of their ministry was the belief that people matter because they are created in the image of God. They also realized that people had struggles and misplaced priorities because the image of God was damaged in the fall. Therefore, their life and ministry worked to restore the lives of people that had been damaged by the fall. These beliefs led them to care for people who had been forgotten. It also led them to create structures that would help disciple people and create healthy, flourishing communities.

The work-life principles and structures they created were proven through great opposition and misunderstanding and tested in the worst of human circumstances. When John Wesley died after more than sixty-five years of dedicated service to his neighbors and the world, he was one of England's most respected and loved figures. He taught and lived spiritual principles that were drawn straight from the Bible and that were shaped and applied according to the best knowledge of his day, the wisdom of godly people, and the reality of human experience.

These principles prove that we are happiest, and we help God to make our world a better place, when three powerful dimensions of life are healthy and in proper alignment with each other:

A personal commitment to spiritual well-being. We live out of the riches of our hearts. This results in a commitment to personal discipleship or what Wesley called *works of piety* that flow from our love for God.

A personal intervention with social systems. We help to make the world a better place when we work to create social systems that focus our collective efforts to improve the lot of our community's least powerful members. We are concerned not only with the poor, but the structures that promote a healthy community where people can overcome poverty. These social systems include legal, political, and economic systems that enable the creation of well-being for all. The vast system of exchange that we call "the economy" is a critical element of the stewardship position God has given us. Like work, economic exchange doesn't just move goods around; it creates value and well-being because we serve one another's needs.

A personal engagement with the needs of others. Even before someone is able to make a contribution through work, we are concerned about their needs because they are created in the image of God. These are what Wesley called *works of mercy* that flow from Jesus' command to love our neighbor.

Each of us is at a different stage of our spiritual journey. The Holy Spirit helps us to recognize where we are on the journey and to use our resources wisely. How will our work and our wealth best promote the well-being of our families and the health of our communities? In a sermon on Luke 16:9, John Wesley put it like this:

> [Wealth] is an excellent gift of God, answering the noblest ends. In the hands of his children, it is food for the hungry, drink for the thirsty, raiment for the naked: It gives to the traveller and the stranger where to lay his head. By it we may supply the place of an husband to the widow, and of a father to the fatherless. We may be a defence for the oppressed, a means of health to the sick, of ease to them that are in pain; it may be as eyes to the blind, as feet to the lame; yea, a lifter up from the gates of death! ("The Use of Money," 2)

The Parts of This Book

Throughout the chapters of this little book we will explore the way that Wesleyan discipleship principles shape the way we think about work, economy, society, and the way we conduct ourselves in these realms. The chapters work their way through two questions:

1. *Who has God called us to be?*
   When God's grace makes us deeply committed and transformed followers of Jesus Christ, how does this transformation show up in the way we work?

2. *What has God called us to do?*
   When we embrace the work to which God has called us, in the way God disciples us to work, how does this discipleship shape the way we care for ourselves and our communities so that God employs our work to make the world a better place?

John Wesley was captivated by the truth that we are shaped in God's image—every single one of us. Each one of us carries an identity shaped by our family DNA and the place and time in which we live. But most importantly, we share the identity that God has given us. We have a calling that is our own unique purpose in life.

The great Wesleyan movement drew on this truth and proved great principles that help us understand the way that God uses work to make us better people and to make the world a better place for all.

The Collaborators

This little primer is the product of a collaboration between a small team of researchers and writers. I, David Wright, have served as the primary architect and author of the primer. Most of the words here are mine, so I take responsibility for any of the weaknesses in the text. The reader should assume that personal pronouns in the text refer to me except as indicated in the sections below (part

1 and in chapters 4 and 5). For quotations from sermons by John Wesley, I have edited and paraphrased his eighteenth-century English for modern English eyes and ears; I have also parenthetically indicated reference locators and cited sermon and other sources in the further reading sections and in the bibliography at the back.

The primer would simply not exist without the contributions of the rest of the team.

Rebecca Whitesel is an award-winning journalist, editor, and publicist who specializes in public relations and human interest stories. Few people research and tell stories about real people better than Rebecca. She researched and wrote the personal vignettes and stories that give such life to the text. She also collected the Wesley quotes and wrote most of the reflection questions.

Christin Taylor is a lifelong Wesleyan and a gifted writer and teacher. She holds the master of fine arts in writing from Antioch University Los Angeles. She teaches writing at Gettysburg College and through her own Blank Page Writing Workshops. Christin provided much of the book's underlying research on current workplace issues. She wrote part 1, "Why Work and Economics Matter," and researched and wrote several sections of chapter 4, "Work That Promotes Personal Well-Being." At several crucial points she provided key insights that helped to shape the structure and direction of the book.

Patrick Eby is one of the freshest and best-informed current scholars on the history and theology of the early Methodist movement. He recently completed his doctoral research at Drew University and now teaches at Indiana Wesleyan University and Asbury Theological Seminary. Patrick provided priceless insights and guidance on specific Wesleyan content and provided drafts of several of the sections that deal with the Wesleyan movement. He provided many of the resources for further reading.

Keith Reeves holds a PhD from Union Theological Seminary, is a professor of New Testament and early Christian literature at

Azusa Pacific University, and is an ordained minister in the Wesleyan Church. He also holds an MBA and is involved in a number of business ventures. He and his wife, Karen, reside in La Verne, California and have three daughters. Keith wrote drafts of several concepts in chapter 5, "Work That Promotes Social and Economic Well-Being."

The primer would also not exist without the guidance, insight, and encouragement of Dwight Gibson. His overall vision for the primer, and his insightful feedback, has been indispensable. I am in his debt for the invitation to create this book. I am also indebted to Dr. Bob Whitesel, Dr. Chris Bounds, and Dr. John Drury for their generous insights into the nuances of Wesleyan theology and their encouragement for this project.

We collectively offer it as our work, done to help others as it may, and to bring glory to God as he wills.

We hope you will enjoy taking this short journey of discovery with us.

David Wright

Why Work and Economics Matter

Faith, mighty faith, the promise sees,
And looks to that alone;
Laughs at impossibilities,
And cries, "It shall be done!"

Charles Wesley

In 2004 my friend Katei Kirby, an intelligent, articulate, and compelling woman from a working-class Caribbean family in London, found herself thrust into Britain's halls of power.

"It was just unprecedented. I would go to Buckingham Palace one week, then Parliament the next, then the United Nations. You think 'hold on a minute,' this is all a bit size 9s and I'm only a size 8," Katei exclaimed with a laugh that bubbles like soda.

As the chief executive of the Afro-Caribbean Evangelical Association (ACEA) it was Katei's responsibility to represent evangelical Christians from African and Caribbean countries to the broader British public. At the time, the African and Caribbean churches were the fastest growing sector of the Christian community in the United Kingdom. They were "seeing phenomenal growth," Katei told me. "And they were doing the most unconventional things like taking over warehouses and cinemas" as their places of worship, she said.

As a result, Christians from African and Caribbean families were garnering lots of attention from the media, and not always good attention.

Katei still remembers the first big negative story that blew up in the press after she took the job. "It was an alleged child abuse case, not sexual abuse, but witchcraft. [The news shows] spun another story that these black Christians were torturing children in the name of their faith."

Ironically, this was exactly the kind of story Katei had told the consultant who trained her that she didn't want to talk about. "Child abuse just angers me, and I said I wouldn't want to talk about that."

But the child abuse case broke and who got to talk to the media? Katei.

Katei did four to six live television interviews, so that way they would not be able to edit her comments. She prayed and asked God for wisdom. When the moment came she delivered her answer. "Yes, awful things are happening, but not in the name of God, and certainly not in the name of the evangelical church," she told the public.

As a result of this story, and Katei's deft handling of the subject matter, the ACEA became a reference point for the media. "We were given opportunities in the BBC and press to put stuff out there and that was all God," explained Katei. She felt she had been given a commission: "Don't just talk to Christians. Tell the world how good God is. I had the chance to do that every day, not always in media, but also behind the scenes."

Not only was Katei's job significant in its subject matter and responsibilities, but also in its position. Until Katei took the job, men had always held her position. She was the first woman to serve as the spokesperson for the African and Caribbean church communities to the British public.

She loved her work. Katei is a gracious, articulate, polished leader. Circles of gracious influence widened from her as effortlessly as ripples in a pool. She worked tirelessly and buoyantly at her work.

Then, suddenly, her work came to a shuddering halt. She found herself laid off because of lack of funding.

"The day the trustees informed me of their decision, I had been in meetings in Westminster exploring opportunities for political engagement," Katei wrote in her frank and beautifully written article for *Christianity* magazine. "The decision had been made," the trustees told her.

The economic downturn which left 2.4 million of Katei's fellow citizens unemployed in 2010 yanked the rug out from underneath the ACEA as well. They could no longer afford to run their operations. A week after Katei was notified that she was being let go, they closed their doors.

And so in a matter of days, Katei went from interceding in the highest halls of British political power to being out of work. A journey of profound challenge awaited her. What would happen next? For the first time in her life, Katei had been fired.

The Bruising Consequences of Losing One's Work

Katei wrote, "I call redundancy an octopus. Over time, it wrapped its tentacles around eight important areas of my life—my identity, my faith, my income, my home, my diet, my health, my wardrobe and my self-worth—and squeezed."

The following year and a half was a time of profound soul-searching for Katei. She found her identity sliced away in pieces.

"I lost my home of seven years, losing with it the sanctuary and security that I had enjoyed there, along with all the joys and freedom of being independent," she said in the article.

From having to alter her diet, to her wardrobe, to having to rely on the generosity of friends and family to help meet her physical needs, Katei felt the final blow of her job loss when she felt herself losing her place in society.

"We list all these things after our name that are activities and it's when I was made redundant, that I was out of work and not by choice, that there was nothing to say after my name," Katei later told me while reflecting on that dark time.

"That silence was loud to me. To me it said, 'And you're useless' or 'You're not useful; therefore you have no identity.'"

It was in this process of loss and grief that Katei began to parse out her old relationship to work.

"I hadn't separated in my head that what I was doing was not who I was. It was simply an opportunity to make effective what I knew. That's not who I was. That was what I was doing. The first twenty to twenty-five years of my working life, there was an eclipse of those two things."

She had to ask herself the difficult question of what she had been attached to and put her identity in before losing her job.

"Some of it was those opportunities," Katei explained. "The sense of feeling useful, valued, and rewarded. God began to tell me quite clearly that those could come without the titles. I could be useful without going to 10 [Downing Street], if I'm willing to do it with the right motives."

Telling Her Story

Katei decided to write her story as a way to answer the difficult questions that crowded into her life along with the loss of her work.

"Where is God in the midst of redundancy?"

"How can the church meet the needs of the unemployed?"

Katei said that the first time she sat down to write her story she "cried like a baby." She wrote with a face "full of tears," but the experience was a healing process. She sent her story off to the editors of *Christianity* magazine, who published her story nearly untouched by edits.

Coincidentally, or providentially, by the time her article was published, Katei had found a new job. "God had provided me work," she joyfully reported.

Katei is working for the Methodist Church of Great Britain, addressing the issue of integration (or lack thereof) in the church. Much like her last job, Katei's work requires her to communicate and interface between communities within and outside of the church.

"What I'm working on is called, 'Belonging Together,' and it's an opportunity to address some of the barriers that keep people [of color from] coming forward into places of leadership."

Katei has been tasked with understanding what perpetuates the imbalance of power and how to help open the doors to all congregants, regardless of color, to more easily serve in the church.

In a wonderful twist of the story, Katei is back in the places of power she once visited. "I'm back in Whitewall, but with a totally different approach," she noted. "These are just opportunities to engage. If there's an issue to be aware of, I've been tasked with the opportunity to go and inform, go provide useful and relevant information so they can make good decisions."

Why Work and Economics Matter

What did Katei learn from her journey through the experience of being without work? She learned just how deeply work mattered to every aspect of her well-being.

Though she has the privilege of working in the halls of power, Katei says she no longer thinks of her work in terms of status. Her approach to work was altered because of her journey through loss, grief, reflection, and growth.

Now she knows that her work is about something completely different. With her costly but cherished new insight, she now says, "I want to be a good disciple, a good steward of what God's put inside me, my talent, my time."

Work, productivity, and economic security weave their way through our lives, identities, and spirituality. We can see ourselves in Katei's admission of the sway that her work held over her sense of worth and well-being. Who among us can say that the tasks we apply ourselves to day in and day out do not in some way give us a sense of value, a sense of purpose? Work permeates the very core of our being.

All too often we reject the notion that work shapes our identity. We feel we should discipline ourselves into viewing it otherwise, but perhaps to do so is simply to run against the grain of what God has intended. Perhaps, it is part of his good and perfect will that we should love our work, and that it should inform every aspect of our lives. Perhaps it is not sinful or "bad" that work gives us a sense of power, a sense of forward movement, a sense of connection, a sense of well-being. Because we are made in the image of a creating God, our work does quite a bit more than just occupy our time or provide basic necessities; it creates value for people, so wealth and well-being can grow over time.

Perhaps the key is, rather than viewing these influences of work as ends in and of themselves, we should view them as a part of God's work in our lives and what he is doing in the world for those around us, for the kingdom, and for the resurrected creation. The fact that we gain a sense of power from our work is not power to meet our own needs and fragile egos, but power to serve those less privileged than ourselves. The reality that work creates structure for our time and our future is not meant purely for our own successful climb "up the ladder," but is meant to create space and balance in our lives so we can give time to our families, our churches, our friends, our communities. Perhaps the truth that work stretches beyond just ourselves into our social networks and gives us a sense of worth is not just for our own benefit and well-being, but is so we may influence those around us and move them not only closer to personal well-being, but closer to God.

Our work provides for our physical needs. It gives us a sense of purpose and worth. Work informs our sense of self, the stories we tell about ourselves and our place in the world. Work defines our place in society. In many ways, it places us on "the grid" that holds civilization together. Work gives us our sense of forward progress. It creates a framework for our future, a structure on which to hang our plans, our dreams, our hopes.

Our work is embedded inextricably within a social network that most of us do not think about very often. In fact, when we face the kind of cataclysmic personal upheaval that Katei experienced with the loss of her work, we often tend to think about the immediate and personal circumstances and causes of that loss.

One of the greatest contributions of the great Wesleyan movement was that John Wesley offered two insights that we will explore throughout this book. First, he knew that a strong personal connection to the transforming power of Jesus Christ would give individuals strength and dignity in the face of these cataclysmic events. So he worked hard to introduce people to the personal transformation of meeting and knowing Christ. Second, he also knew that our experience of work is embedded deeply within the larger social network of the economy, which in turn is shaped by the legal and political structures of a society. So he personally worked hard to shape those legal, political, and economic decisions. And he called on the people of the Wesleyan movement to give thought and effort to the shaping of the economy in ways that honored biblical principles and brought well-being to the most people. John Wesley knew that government helps the economy flourish when it safeguards the rule of law and personal liberties, ensures fair play, and expands opportunity for people to become self-supporting and successful.

Katei's experience shows us just how integrally our work connects us to the larger social network of the economy. Economic well-being is not some disembodied theoretical reality, argued over by economists and politicians. Work is connected to the well-being of the economy. This is what keeps us in our jobs and provides us with the vehicles by which we use our God-given gifts and talents to bless others. Katei's experience reminds us powerfully of the personal well-being that our work affords to us, and that disappears when the social network of the economy falters. Much of our sense of well-being comes from our ability to earn our way in this world, and that ability depends on the health of the social system that we call the economy.

But there is another equally important dimension for us to see in Katei's story. In Katei's story we see that her work mattered because through her work God was making the world a better place. The benefit of her work was not only for her. It was for those she served. When this service was lost, Katei lost her connection to a greater sense of purpose.

Most importantly, work informs our sense of who God is and shapes our relationship with our Creator. We are thrust into a moment where we must ask where God exists in and around our experience of work, and how we can join the work he is already doing in the world.

Through Katei's story we see that our work matters because through it God provides for our own well-being. But on an even deeper level, our work matters because through it God provides for the well-being of the world.

Reflection Questions

1. If you have lost your work, or experienced that loss with a close friend or relative, how did this experience affect you and them?

2. What are the greatest personal challenges that people experience when they lose their work?

3. What do you believe are the greatest reasons why work and economics matter?

For Further Study

Kirby, Katei. "Where Do You Go from Here?" *Christianity.* September 2010, 40–46. http://www.christianitymagazine.co.uk/Browse%20By%20Category/features/Wheredoyougofromhere.aspx.

How Conversion Transforms the Way We Work

PART 2

In fellowship, alone,
To God, with faith, draw near:
Approach his courts, besiege his throne
With all the power of prayer.

Charles Wesley

Those who study what it takes to gain exceptional mastery of any given field have identified something they call the ten-thousand-hour rule. These experts have discovered that it takes ten thousand hours of practice to achieve mastery. Neuroscientist and musician Daniel Levitin puts it this way in his book *This Is Your Brain on Music*:

[T]en thousand hours of practice is required to achieve the level of mastery associated with being a world-class expert—in anything. In study after study, of composers, basketball players, fiction writers, ice skaters, concert pianists, chess players, master criminals, and what have you, this number comes up again and again. Ten thousand hours is the equivalent to roughly three hours per day, or twenty hours per week, of practice over ten years . . . . [N]o one has yet found a case in which true world-class expertise was accomplished in less

> time. It seems that it takes the brain this long to assimilate all
> that it needs to know to achieve true mastery. (197)

For example, Herbert Simon and Kevin Gilmartin studied chess players to learn how the minds of experts work. They discovered that experts hold in their brains a repertoire of about fifty thousand "chunks" of memory—patterns of chess pieces on the board, sequences of moves, strategies, and their outcomes.

These chunks are stored in long-term memory through years of practice and are retrieved when they are needed, based on the meaning that the information has been assigned. Through thousands of hours and years of practice, experts collect thousands of chunks of memory (information) and organize those chunks, not according to superficial rules or schematics, but according to the meaning they were able to assign to the information.

Experts are able to draw on this rich store of knowledge more quickly and more meaningfully than novices. They recognize patterns and accurately draw from long-term memory those pieces of information that allow them to act most appropriately in any given situation.

Novices tend to analyze problems according to surface features—those features that are most easily observable. Experts tend to analyze, categorize, and respond to problems on the basis of the deep structure of the problem.

One of the surprising discoveries they made was that this high-level functioning has less to do with the innate talents of the experts than it does with long immersion in their chosen activity. While it is true that talent is not equally distributed among us, beyond the basic level of talent that any field requires, what separates novices from experts is not talent but purposeful practice.

These observations seem to hold real promise for our practice of whole-life discipleship. When we talk about whole-life discipleship, we are talking about the application of godly principles to every area of our lives, not just to those areas that we typically think of as being "spiritual" in nature.

We certainly should aspire to be the very best at what we do. Might we also aspire to bring to our work a rich expertise in seeing, analyzing, and acting like Jesus?

What if Wesleyans truly embraced the discipleship challenge of becoming experts in two fields—the work to which we are called and the application to that work of the holiness that deep and thorough conversion accomplishes in us?

Discipleship at Work

Discipleship isn't a word that we normally associate with work. It is one of those spiritual words that seem to belong in church. But a disciple is simply a follower of someone. Becoming a disciple of someone means to follow that person, to make that person's vision, values, and priorities one's own.

To be a disciple of Jesus Christ is to be so captivated with Jesus that all of one's life comes to be shaped by the personality, character, and priorities of Jesus.

If it takes ten thousand hours of practice to become an expert, let's assume just for argument's sake that it will take ten thousand hours to become an expert disciple of Jesus Christ.

But where should we invest those ten thousand hours?

Let's think about this for a moment. The first answer that comes to mind is that if I want to become an expert disciple, I should invest those ten thousand hours in spiritual activities like Bible reading, prayer, and worship.

Over my adult lifetime, if I spend four hours a week in church and another six hours a week in personal spiritual disciplines, I will devote about thirteen thousand hours to these specifically spiritual activities.

But the more I think about this, the more I wonder if this is the best way to look at the challenge. This would be a great way to invest my time if being an expert follower of Jesus was all about what I did while I was in church and pursuing my personal spiritual disciplines. But while these certainly seem necessary and rewarding pursuits, my Wesleyan heritage teaches me that this isn't really what makes me an expert disciple of Jesus.

The great Wesleyan revival demonstrated the truth that becoming a disciple of Jesus is just as much about what happens in all the other hours of my life as it is about what happens in the hours I invest in personal spiritual disciplines and in attending church.

So let's look at that part of the equation. Over my adult life I will spend about fifty-two thousand hours working—fifty-two thousand hours in which to learn and apply godly principles to my life's work.

And what if these two arenas of life actually serve to inform one another? What if our mastery of our work is actually enhanced by our mastery of godly principles? What if our mastery of spiritual principles is actually made possible by the effort to apply them to our work? What if it turns out that there is almost no other arena better suited to give us mastery of our discipleship than the arena of our life's work?

This, in fact, is exactly what John Wesley taught. This truth lay at the heart of the Wesleyan way of following Jesus.

Cognitive scientists tell us that experts amass a vast repertoire of experience, categorized by deep structures of meaning, available at a moment's recall from long-term memory, and that they are able to apply that recalled information appropriately to the complex and numberless array of challenges that they encounter.

This is our discipleship challenge at work.

Perhaps holiness is the halo that surrounds us, without our even noticing, when we are living out both our professional and spiritual mastery in the daily grind of life, when we are deciding how to respond in godly and highly professional ways to the tumult of opportunities and challenges that make up real life in the workplace.

Reflection Questions

1. What does the concept of "whole-life discipleship" mean to you?
2. What are the greatest challenges you face in pursing discipleship at work?
3. What resources do you have to inspire and instruct you in creating a discipleship of work?

For Further Reading

Levitin, Daniel. *This Is Your Brain on Music: The Science of a Human Obsession.* New York: Penguin, 2006.

Simon, Herbert, and Kevin J. Gilmartin. "A Simulation of Memory for Chess Positions." *Cognitive Psychology* 5 (1973): 29–46. http://www.cs.wright.edu/~snarayan/isis/pdf/group5one.pdf.

Who God Has Called Us to Be

A charge to keep I have,
A God to glorify;
A never-dying soul to save,
And fit it for the sky.

Charles Wesley

Those who belong to the John Wesley family of churches anchor their perspectives on whole-life discipleship in the truths that were proven through the great Wesleyan revival that started in eighteenth-century England and soon become a global movement.

Millions of people's lives were changed by this movement. Historians say that the Wesleyan revival changed the course of English history. It became the most powerful spiritual force in the emerging American nation, and ultimately became a global community of faith.

At the heart of this great movement that literally changed the world was a simple yet profound message—a message of personal conversion through faith in Jesus Christ.

Throughout his more than sixty-five years of ministry John Wesley, the founder of this great movement, preached, wrote, and taught about conversion more than any other topic. Personal conversion was the great bedrock truth at the heart of a movement that changed the world.

How could this simple message propel a worldwide revolution that transformed peoples' personal lives, helped to abolish slavery, reversed the spread of addiction, helped to humanize brutal industrial working conditions, encouraged the growth of a middle class, addressed inhumane prison practices, and helped to spread education for all?

The Transforming Reality of Conversion

In 1765 John Wesley preached a sermon that became the classic statement of the message of conversion that was at the heart of the Wesleyan revival. The sermon is titled "The Scripture Way of Salvation" and is based on Ephesians 2:8, "You have been saved, through faith."

In this sermon John Wesley argued that salvation, or conversion, is different than what most people think of when they hear the word. Conversion is not about getting ready to go to heaven. It isn't about some nebulous eternal happiness, or the soul's migration to paradise after death.

Here is an excerpt from John Wesley's most famous sermon on salvation. I have edited and paraphrased his eighteenth-century English for modern English ears here and in subsequent quotations of the same kind of material.

> The salvation I am talking about is not what religious people frequently understand the word to mean.
>
> I am not talking about going to heaven, or eternal happiness, or the soul's going to paradise. The salvation I mean is not a blessing which lies on the other side of death. It is not something at a distance.

Instead, salvation is a present thing, a blessing which, through the free mercy of God, we can possess here and now. It includes everything God does to draw us into a relationship with himself.

God shines the light of truth in this world and that light prompts us to do what is just and merciful and humble. All of this is God's grace. If we respond to it, God leads us toward salvation. Unfortunately, most of us stifle these desires and turn away from this light.

The way to salvation is to respond to God's call. We receive this salvation through faith . . .

When we experience this salvation the power of God makes us new inside. We feel the love of God in our hearts. It spreads through our whole being changing everything about us.

It makes us love other people, especially other children of God.

It squeezes out the things that we loved before we were saved—the love of the world, the love of pleasure, of ease, of honor, of money.

This love pushes aside our pride, anger, self-will, and every other evil temper. In a word, it changes our earthly, sensual, devilish mindset into a mindset like that of Jesus Christ . . .

We find that we want to turn away from everything that even appears to be evil. Love motivates us to do all the good we can do. We worship God with our hearts and with our actions. We even go so far as to deny ourselves pleasures that may be innocent in themselves but that do not lead us closer to God.

In this way, we wait for God to sanctify us entirely, a full salvation from all our sins, from pride, self-will, anger, and unbelief. As the Apostle put it, we press on toward perfection.

But what is perfection? Is this a healthy, or even a possible pursuit?

The word has various meanings, but applied to our relationship with God, perfection means perfect love. It is love that excludes sin, love filling the heart, taking up the whole capacity of the soul. It is a kind of love that makes us joyful people, that makes prayer a constant companion, and that makes us approach life with thankfulness. ("The Scripture Way of Salvation," I.1–2, 4, 8–9)

The great Wesleyan movement that changed millions of lives and made a profound impact on the world started with this experience of deep personal transformation.

John Wesley wasn't just preaching about a set of intellectual beliefs to which he wanted people to give their assent. He didn't start by calling people to an agenda for social action. He wasn't asking them to take positions on issues, though transformed people would eventually do all of those things. No, John Wesley first wanted to introduce his neighbors to something both simpler and more profound. He wanted them to come to know Jesus Christ, to enter a personal relationship that would completely change the way they thought, what they loved, and how they would act.

John Wesley called his neighbors to something he had experienced—a complete change of life that grew from a profound sense of forgiveness and a radical change of heart. This is what he called *salvation*. Salvation is not a word that means much to us today. A more common concept that is really more faithful to John Wesley's genius is the word *conversion*. The goal of the profound personal conversion that John Wesley called his neighbors to experience is a perfect love of God and a perfect love of our neighbors. This deep experience of conversion starts with personal acceptance of God's call.

A Strange Way to Change the World

You have to love the sheer improbability of the way God used this salvation message preached in 1765 to change the world. One of the greatest lessons John Wesley's movement taught the world is that before we ask *what* we are called *to do*, we must first ask *who* we are called *to be*. Before we act we must come to terms with who we are.

The Industrial Revolution was creating spectacular new wealth. It would eventually create engines of shared wealth such as the world had never before seen. But this positive outcome had not yet become apparent. The vast majority of Wesley's neighbors lived in squalor and even brutality. The abuses of the system were all too evident:

- The laws of the land favored the rich and powerful.
- Education was available to only the most privileged.
- People were moving from the countryside into the cities. Work and family norms were changing faster than people could cope.
- The centers of intellectual life were actively discrediting the accepted truths of the past and embracing new and controversial ideas.
- The church was irrelevant and disengaged from the crushing burdens of the common people.
- Infant mortality was shockingly high. Alcoholism was commonplace. Work was hard, dangerous, and poorly paid. Violence against children was all too common.

These were the sorts of problems, along with other factors, that led neighboring France to descend into the violence of the French Revolution.

However, something amazing happened in England. Wesley went around the country preaching about conversion, organizing people into small groups to nurture their growth as followers of Jesus Christ, and promoting the cause of helping those who were least able to help themselves. England began to change.

The movement that grew from John Wesley's preaching attacked these problems with a balance that has been sadly lacking in our society today. He preached a message of personal conversion and created communities of accountability. He preached both personal responsibility and then helped people who had experienced this profound reorientation of their lives to develop systems that would help care for the neighbors. He worked on the local level, but also wrote letters to those in leadership asking for changes that would make life better for those who suffered under oppressive circumstances.

Wesley rode horseback more than 250,000 miles back and forth across England to communicate the message he believed people needed to hear. In each town he set up societies that would not only care for the spiritual growth of their members, but would also care for those in need whether or not they belonged to the new societies. In other words, Wesleyans reached out to care for people in need regardless of what they believed or where they belonged—as Christians they reached out to people as human beings.

Wesley addressed those in the government when he thought government policies needed to change. Two letters in particular illustrate his approach. He wrote an open letter criticizing the use of grains to provide luxury items while others went without food. In another letter, his last letter, he encouraged British politician William Wilberforce to keep fighting for the freedom of the slaves.

He formed charitable organizations to meet the needs of the least fortunate. John and his brother Charles played a major role in the formation of an orphanage in the province of Georgia in the American colonies and a school for the children of the poor called Kingswood school in the Bristol area of England.

The revival that changed England and the world eventually used every tool it could find to live out the aspiration of perfect love for God and neighbor. People whose lives had been changed by their saving encounter with Jesus Christ used political power, economic might, and social connections to try to make the world a better place.

But this great movement didn't start there. The Wesleyan revival began when people recognized that they were people created in the image of God, and thus called to live lives of meaning and purpose. They were called to lives of immeasurable impact once their hearts and minds were transformed by the work of the Holy Spirit through the message of conversion.

Bitterness of Heart

An old Yiddish proverb says, "If there is bitterness in the heart, sugar in the mouth won't make life sweeter." Perhaps one of the great lessons of the Wesleyan movement is that if there is bitterness in the heart, the work of our hands will inevitably produce division, conflict, and need. But if there is love and holiness in our hearts, then our hands may produce well-being and peace.

Our assumptions about work these days are badly skewed. All too often, our baseline assumption about our work is that it is a kind of penalty, a curse laid upon us for the bitterness that came into the world through sin. Or we think of work as the means by which we amass wealth that we can use to provide for our own security and to buy the material possessions that will make us happy.

We think that when our work produces wealth it will assuage the bitterness in our hearts. But our Wesleyan heritage teaches us a very different kind of discipleship. When we are deeply, truly, thoroughly transformed by faith in Jesus Christ, the Holy Spirit begins to draw away the bitterness that has crippled our hearts for so long. Like a poison drawn out of a pulsing wound, the bitterness of estrangement, suspicion, fear, and selfishness is drawn away and displaced by the joy and peace of a living relationship with Jesus.

Just as he changed the lives of those who met him on the streets and in the first-century living rooms of Jerusalem, Jesus changes us when we meet him in the hustle and bustle, technoculture, and ambiguity of our late modern world.

When we really meet Jesus, we cannot help but see the brokenness of our own hearts. Yet unlike the criticisms of even our most well-meaning friends, when we meet Jesus we see our sins not as brutal blows of shame, but as moments for repentance and surrender, as markers for the great possibility of becoming something we never could have dreamed. Jesus calls us out of the bitterness of brokenness to the promise of wholeness and hope.

When we walk in company with Jesus we begin a journey of complete life transformation that leads to peace with ourselves, and love for God and our neighbors. When this change of heart makes its way into our work and economic activity, work takes on a whole new meaning. We come to work as changed people, and work comes to us in a whole new way.

Reflection Questions

1. What do you believe is the most intriguing aspect of John Wesley's concept of conversion?

2. Have you experienced the kind of conversion that is described in this chapter? If so, how has that experience changed your life?

3. Have you had the experience of having God change "bitterness of heart" that you might have carried with you? If so, how did that happen for you, and what have you learned from the experience?

For Further Reading

Heitzenrater, Richard P. *Wesley and the People Called Methodists.* Nashville: Abingdon, 1995.

Noll, Mark A. *The Rise of Evangelicalism: The Age of Edwards, Whitefield, and the Wesleys.* History of Evangelicalism 1. Downers Grove, IL: Inter-Varsity, 2003.

Wesley, John. "The Scripture Way of Salvation." Ephesians 2:8 (sermon, n.p., 1765). In *Sermons of John Wesley, 1872 Edition.* Edited by Thomas Jackson. Wesley Center Online. http://wesley.nnu.edu/john -wesley/the-sermons-of-john-wesley-1872-edition/sermon-43-the -scripture-way-of-salvation/. The text for John Wesley's sermons here and in all subsequent citations originally came from the Christian Classics Ethereal Library, www.ccel.org.

People of Assurance | 1

I felt I did trust in Christ, Christ alone,
for salvation; and an assurance was given me
that He had taken away my sins, even mine.

John Wesley

Let's return, for a moment, to Katei Kirby's story of loss and discovery. Beneath the brutal circumstances of Katei's journey was a bedrock truth that served as the unshakable foundation of her life. Beneath the hurt and confusion, beneath the layers of loss, was a deep principle of assurance that held Katei steady as she tumbled through the disorienting experience of losing her job and all that went with it.

The fact is, we never know when we will face a journey like Katei's. Even in good times work is not without its challenges. To face the tumult of the world we need a foundation of confidence on which to stand.

We simply cannot succeed in the work God has called us to do unless we can first become the persons God has called us to be. We will not succeed in our life's calling if our inner lives are divided, uncertain, and conflict ridden.

Insecurity and fear are terrible burdens to carry into our work. Am I good enough? Will I succeed? Will I be liked? Will I be supported? Will I be strong enough to survive when things aren't easy, or fair, or just, or good?

Life blows the difficult circumstances we face out of all proportion. Will I have what I need? Will I be given the opportunity to succeed? Will others conspire against me? Will the challenges I face prove too much for me to overcome?

Life fixes our focus on debilitating comparisons with others and overburdens our minds with concerns about what others think of us. Will they approve? Will they give me a chance? Will they recognize my gift? Will they betray me? Will they respect me?

One of the greatest principles that Wesley taught was that the assurance of true and deep and thoroughgoing conversion gives us the confidence to do our work with purpose, conviction, and also humility.

Wesley showed us that we are called to be persons of assurance. And because we are people at rest in the assurance of true conversion, we can carry into our work the quiet confidence that lets others be themselves, sure of our convictions and content to face whatever consequences those convictions bring, and content in the knowledge that God puts us where we are to make his contribution of goodwill and blessing to the lives of others.

This certainly does not mean that work will be easy, that we will not face pressure and perplexity. Godly people carry all the emotions with which God has stocked our human nature. But in the midst of challenge is when we come to see that there is no assurance that compares to the confidence that comes with knowing that we are truly, fully, and completely saved by the love of Jesus, that we are empowered by God's Spirit, that we are known and loved unconditionally, fully and finally accepted in the presence of God.

God's love for us has no end and it is not earned by our performance. It is deeper, richer, and more sophisticated than our imagination can conceive. God loves us in ways we have not yet discovered.

God's acceptance of us has no limits. It is not dependent on the color of our skin, the language we speak, the place of our birth, the culture of our upbringing or the wealth of our family. It does not depend on the profundity of our religious insights or the perfection of our spiritual performance.

John Wesley showed us that when Wesleyans go to work, we go with our sins forgiven, our failures redeemed, our imperfections anointed by the influence of God's grace, our focus on others, and our eyes on the prize of making the world a better place. This echoes the words of divine assurance spoken through the prophet Isaiah (43:1–3), in which God says,

> Fear not, for I have redeemed you;
>> I have summoned you by name; you are mine.
> When you pass through the waters,
>> I will be with you;
> and when you pass through the rivers,
>> they will not sweep over you.
> When you walk through the fire,
>> you will not be burned;
>> the flames will not set you ablaze.
> For I am the LORD, your God,
>> the Holy One of Israel, your Savior.

Who are Wesleyans called to be at work? We along with all other Christians are called to be persons of assurance.

Human achievement, no matter how great, always brings a fleeting assurance. The moment we win, the question becomes, can we win again? Any assurance built on our own achievements seeps away through the cracks of this imperfect world in which we live. Sooner or later we are left with the same old gnawing doubts and fears.

But the assurance that God gives us is a gift. No one ever got this assurance by trying harder. We get it by faith in Jesus Christ, by living in the reality of that relationship day by day.

Being a person of assurance does not change the circumstances of our work. But it gives us endurance in the face of those circumstances. It does not change the basic abilities we bring to our work. But it gives us the certainty that God will use our abilities to make a difference.

Having the assurance that comes from God does not change the reality that injustice will invade the place we work. But it gives us the passion to challenge and transform the ugliness of injustice through the beauty of truth, stubborn love, and forgiveness.

Living with God's assurance in our hearts does not remove the threats that bring fear into our work. But it gives us courage to call those fears the brazen imposters that they are, and courage to take a step forward when everything tells us to run away.

God's gift of assurance does not remove the temptation to be preoccupied with ourselves at work. But it gives us the vision to see the needs of others and the commitment to bring well-being to those around us.

Professor Wilbur Williams is one of those Christians in the Wesleyan family whose life embodies the assurance of conversion, the assurance of knowing who God has created him to be, the assurance that God will not only supply his needs but through creativity and consistent work, an abundance from which to bless others. Most of all, the fact that Wilbur and his lovely wife, Ardelia, are people of deep assurance gives them the security to build a lifetime of work around an investment in relationships that serve others.

> In souls filled with love, the desire to please God is a continual prayer.
>
> John Wesley

Professor of the Year

At the age of eighty-two, Dr. Wilbur Williams is still teaching a full load. The legendary associate professor of biblical literature and archaeology at Indiana Wesleyan University accepts just $1 a year from his employment. And, students continually select him their Professor of the Year.

"Yes, I teach for $1 a year," he admitted. "I had one student say, 'I thought you were boasting!' and I said, 'Oh, you don't know me! That would be the farthest thing from my mind.'" Wilbur has the Lord's interests in mind.

"When we got married we were so poor we could not afford a hamburger outside of the house. My wife had a little bit of debt left and it was hard for me to try to go on to graduate school," he relayed. But they committed themselves to God and his plan for their lives, and went to work.

John Wesley thought Christians should be industrious and their hard work would yield financial gain. This principle has proven to be true in Wilbur's life.

The first real estate profit came quite unexpectedly. Purchasers defaulted on a loan for a house sold by his elderly parents. They were too old to repossess it, so the bank offered it to Wilbur for $700, divesting all interest. He fixed it up, rented it for $90 a month, then sold it for $7,500 eight years later. He parceled the money into $1,000 increments and started buying houses around the campus to rent or resell.

It was amazing when the right properties came for sale, but "as always, I went to prayer about it and felt a green light or red light . . . I will not buy or sell until I have prayed about every decision," Wilbur emphatically stated. After teaching all day he would put on work clothes and go fix a problem . . . "termites, toilets that didn't work, drains that needed to be cleaned . . . Now I hire the work done!" He smiled.

For years the Williamses have been supported through property investment income. Meanwhile, they have given many annuities, built a prayer chapel and commissioned statues around campus and at the Wesleyan Church headquarters, supported those going to the mission field, and led 152 Spiritual Odyssey tours to Israel.

"I want to give God the glory—we were so poor. I'm always shaking my head, how did I do it?" He credits his mother who taught him to tithe even when the family was so poor they never tasted fresh bread or milk.

Wilbur finds his greatest satisfaction in relationships. "I love my wife more now than ever," he declared about the love of his life, who coordinated Indiana Wesleyan University's art department for thirty-five years before retiring in 2002.

He also loves students. "They know I love them, I tell them so. I can talk straight to the students . . . they appreciate me being honest with them . . . I'm not here to say how great a scholar I am—I don't even think that—and I'm not working for Professor of the Year. I'm working for the Lord. But the beautiful thing is God enabled me to do it without being paid."

Wilbur and Ardelia are living examples of John Wesley's famous Covenant Prayer. Each year John Wesley and his followers would remember that God was in control and they could live in the midst of all of the struggles and pressures of being employed or unemployed.

> I am no longer my own, but thine. Put me to what thou wilt, rank me with whom thou wilt. Put me to doing, put me to suffering. Let me be employed for thee or laid aside for thee, exalted for thee or brought low for thee. Let me be full, let me be empty. Let me have all things, let me have nothing. I freely and heartily yield all things to thy pleasure and disposal. And now O glorious and blessed God, Father, Son, and Holy Spirit, thou art mine, and I am thine. So be it. And the

covenant which I have made on earth, let it be ratified in heaven. Amen. (As used ⁓ ⁓k of *Offices* of the British Methodist Church, 19?

Reflection Questions

1. What hard sit⟨
2. How did you ⟨
3. How would ⟨
   ents itself?

For Further ⟨

Clapper, Gregory ⟨. ⟨
   ville: Upper Room Books, ⟨

Methodist Church of Great Britain. *The Book* ⟨ ⟨ *s of Service Authorized for Use in the Methodist Church* ⟨ ⟨ *the Order of Morning Prayer.* London: Methodist Publishing House, 1936.

Yrigoyen, Charles, Jr. *John Wesley: Holiness of Heart and Life.* Nashville: Abingdon, 1996. See especially chapters 1–3.

People of Integrity | 2

Along with divine assurance, another principle that deep and thorough conversion awakens in us is the principle of integrity.

Our world has awakened to the desperate need for a renewal of ethics in the workplace. When people do not act ethically, trust is broken. When trust is broken the typical response is to pass new laws, create new regulations, and put in place watchdog people, agencies, and processes.

Meanwhile trust erodes further. Attention is diverted from productive work to the task of compliance. Precious resources are spent not on the purpose of one's enterprise but on the task of complying with regulations. In the end, the genuine pursuit of ethical behavior is buried beneath a mountain of rules that come to be identified with ethics. Economies flourish when people have integrity and trust each other. The original desire for open, honorable, mutually beneficial, and trustworthy interactions gets lost in a deadening legal and regulatory maze.

A modern dictionary defines *integrity* as "adherence to moral and ethical principles; soundness of moral character; honesty" (*Dictionary.com Unabridged*, 2012). An etymological dictionary notes that the word originated about 1400 and first meant "innocence, blamelessness; chastity, purity." By the mid-1400s it began to be used to denote "wholeness, perfect condition." According to an earlier edition of the same etymological dictionary, by the mid-1500s the word *integrity* carried the meaning of "uncorrupted virtue" (*Online Etymology Dictionary*, 2012; ibid. on *Dictionary.com*, 2010).

One of the great principles that John Wesley's ministry demonstrated is that people of integrity work from an internal motivation to act morally and ethically, regardless of the circumstances, and even in the face of great odds. People of integrity always seek to find and do what is right.

Wesley often preached about the transformation that God's love makes in our hearts. In a sermon on Romans 3:31 he said that when God's love reigns in our hearts, it is as though God establishes his law within us so that we do out of love what the law requires out of duty.

> There is no other motive that so powerfully draws us to love God as the certainty of the love God has shown us in Jesus Christ. Nothing enables us to give our hearts to him like the piercing conviction of his love for us.
>
> This principle of grateful love to God gives birth to our own genuine love for our brothers and sisters. Indeed, we can scarcely avoid loving our neighbors when we are truly immersed in God's love for us.
>
> Now this love for our neighbors, grounded in our faith in and love for God, causes us to "do no harm to our neighbor." As the Apostle observes, "love is the fulfillment of the negative law." By this he means that the laws such as these, "Thou shalt not commit adultery, Thou shalt not kill, Thou

shalt not steal, Thou shalt not bear false witness, Thou shalt not covet," are all included in the command, "Thou shalt love thy neighbor as thyself."

Genuine love is not content just to refrain from doing harm to our neighbor. Instead love motivates us to do good at every opportunity, in every possible way, and to every possible degree, to everyone we can.

God's love that fills up our hearts to overflowing through faith is the fulfilling of both the positive and the negative law of God.

This kind of faith doesn't only lead us to fulfill the law in our actions toward others, it also changes the inner landscape of our lives by purifying our hearts from the unworthy and destructive affections that cause us so much grief. The Bible says that "Everyone that has this faith purifies himself, just as God is pure"—purifies himself from every earthly sensual desire, from all vile and inordinate affections. Indeed this love purifies us from the whole carnal mindset that lives in opposition against God. If we allow the love of God to do its perfect work, it fills us with all goodness, righteousness, and truth. It brings all of heaven into our lives so that we live our lives in the brilliant light of God's presence. ("The Law Established through Faith: Discourse Two," III.3–4)

A deeper meaning of the word *integrity* is "the state of being whole, entire, or undiminished." To have integrity is to be "sound, unimpaired, or [in] perfect condition" (*Dictionary.com Unabridged*, 2012).

Perhaps a lack of integrity, then, comes about because of something lacking, something missing, in our being. In fact, it is amazing how often a lack of integrity can be traced to fear, jealousy, greed, and other dishonorable motivations. We lack some fundamental sense of well-being, wholeness, or authenticity in our innermost beings, and so we act in ways that compromise our integrity and destroy our neighbors. Soon laws and regulations spring up to protect us from each other and from ourselves.

As opposed to this outside-in approach—an approach that never truly produces what it seeks—integrity in the Wesleyan way of thinking comes from an inside-out approach.

Imagine the transformational effect on an organization if all of the people in the organization worked from a dedication to act with integrity. What if the words we spoke about one another in the workplace were unfailingly words of integrity? What if the way we treated one another in the workplace was unfailingly honorable? What if the way we treated customers and clients was unfailingly honest and in their best interest?

Imagine the transformational effect on a culture, a society, and a nation if the people of that society adopted the truly radical commitment to live out a social ethic based on such virtues as truthfulness, fairness, and self-control. Impossible to measure is the terrible price we pay when integrity erodes from our personal and public lives.

Integrity builds trust. Trust builds the strength of a nation. Stephen M. R. Covey in *The Speed of Trust* wrote,

> Trust in almost every social institution (government, media, business, health care, churches, political parties, etc.) is significantly lower than a generation ago, and in many cases, sits at historic lows. . . .
>
> Perhaps even more telling is the loss of trust with regard to people trusting other people. A recent survey conducted by British sociologist David Halpern reveals that only 34% of Americans believe that other people can be trusted. In Latin America, the number is only 23%, and in Africa, the figure is 18%. Halpern's research also shows that four decades ago in Great Britain, 60% of the population believed other people could be trusted; today, it's down to 29%. (10–11)

Mistrust hampers the ability of politicians to govern, ties up the nation's courts in a deluge of needless litigation, and cripples the economy through rafts of regulation and security precautions whose only purpose is a failing attempt to legislate integrity. The great British journalist and essayist G. K. Chesterton once made this wise observation:

> When you break the big laws, you do not get liberty; you do not even get anarchy. You get the small laws.

Today, our personal lives and our social networks are dying the death of a thousand small laws brought into existence by our refusal to become people of integrity. Economies flourish when goodwill is universal and global, but control is local and personal knowledge guides decisions.

This inside-out approach for exhibiting integrity and building trust is the ideal that Wesley held up for his spiritual progeny to pursue in their personal lives, at work, and in their influence on their society. In fact, according to Wesley, work is one of the greatest arenas we will have in which to work out this kind of holistic discipleship.

But is this really possible? Are there any role models of this kind of Wesleyan discipleship at work? Let us introduce you to Ralph Hodges.

> You have nothing to do but to save souls. Therefore spend and be spent in this work.
>
> John Wesley

A Man of Integrity

When you practice what you believe, people notice, and Ralph Hodges is living proof.

Ralph climbed the ladder of success quickly after completing graduate work at Carnegie Institute of Technology (now Carnegie Mellon University). He was manager of operations research for

Mead Papers, and with Champion Papers before founding his own company, Management Decisions Development Corp. The company specialized in computer applications in the pulp and paper industry. Later it expanded into administrative systems for colleges and universities.

Ralph was a resource person for his business partner, Dr. John F. Pierce, on his doctoral dissertation for MIT, which dealt with a large-scale mathematical problem in paper mill scheduling. John had an extremely high IQ, with three graduate degrees and no concept of faith, Ralph said. "In the process I was able to become involved in his spiritual search . . . He finally took that step [of faith] and he and his wife started a ministry for young single adults that grew to over two-hundred individuals!"

He said, "The US economy was not its best when we started the company in 1969. We were undercapitalized and found it necessary to look off shore to other countries for business." But Ralph trusted God and found favor in the marketplace. For example, once he was impressed not to board a plane home but to visit a prospective client in Amsterdam instead. "It was too early to call and you don't arrive unannounced in Europe," Ralph chuckled. "Yet my contact was very open to my stopping by. I left the Netherlands at 5 pm that day on a flight to New York with a contract and a sizable deposit in hand for four mills!" They had clients all around the world. Ralph's actions that day were rooted in a lifetime of commitment to the integrity of putting clients first, understanding their needs, and seeking their well-being whenever possible.

As a teenager Ralph's then hobby allowed him to become a pilot, which benefited his business in adulthood. "I used the plane to reach out to paper mills, which were not normally built near major cities, particularly in Canada, and to transport prospective customers to mill sites to see our systems in operation. In more than fifty years of flying Ralph accumulated 7,500 hours of accident-free flying.

John Wesley believed in using one's skills and talents to their fullest potential, and this is certainly what Ralph did with his flying expertise.

His company hired many computer science graduates of Nazarene colleges. "Our clients noticed a difference in the way we did business not because we said anything, but because of the way we performed and what we were able to accomplish," Ralph stated.

Denominational leaders noticed his penchant for leadership and integrity, and elected or appointed him to numerous boards and committees, including the General Board of the Church of the Nazarene. He was a longtime member of the Mount Vernon Nazarene University Board of Trustees and gave the lead gift for the university chapel. The R. R. Hodges Chapel is named for Ralph's father, who taught at Nazarene universities.

Ralph and his wife, Ruth, participated in many mission trips, building churches, schools, and homes for pastors in Africa, South America, the Philippines, and the Dominican Republic. He has been retired for many years but stays busy volunteering. "We made many wonderful friends!" he exclaimed. In the process, they enriched many communities physically and spiritually.

Reflection Questions

1. Who do you admire because of their integrity?
2. Name some of the good character traits you see in them.
3. What will you do to become a person of integrity?

For Further Reading

Wesley, John. "The Law Established through Faith: Discourse Two." Romans 3:31 (sermon, n.p., 1750). In *Sermons of John Wesley, 1872 Edition*. Edited by Thomas Jackson. Wesley Center Online. http://wesley.nnu.edu/john-wesley/the-sermons-of-john-wesley-1872-edition/sermon-36-the-law-established-through-faith-discourse-two/.

People of Authenticity |

3

> Forth in Thy name, O Lord, I go,
> My daily labor to pursue;
> Thee, only Thee, resolved to know
> In all I think, or speak, or do.
>
> **Charles Wesley**

Following assurance and integrity, a third principle of discipleship that was proven in the great Wesleyan movement is the principle of authenticity.

We think of authenticity as being "true to one's own personality, spirit, or character" (*Merriam-Webster Online Dictionary*, 2012). The radical individualism that grows from this philosophy is one of the most powerful messages of our time. It is a mantra that guides our personal choices, and shapes our political, economic, social, and even spiritual life.

But this individualistic sense of trying to be authentic is misleading. It is one of the seductive lies that, far from bringing the happiness it promises, only deepens the bitterness in our hearts. There is another, truer, way to think of authenticity.

Here is a fact about the concept of authenticity. Something that is authentic is said to "conform to an original so as to reproduce [the] essential features [of the original]." Something that is authentic is "made or done the same way as an original." To be authentic is to be "real, actual, not false or [an] imitation." It is to be "genuine, trustworthy, and reliable."

Authenticity bestows great worth. When something is said to be authentic, its worth is enhanced. Far from cheapening it, a certificate of authenticity lifts an object up for greater respect. Authenticity generates trust. It assures greater fascination and attraction.

Now here is the interesting thing to notice. By definition, to call something authentic both lifts that object up *while at the same time* pointing at something else beyond the object itself. A certificate of authenticity says, "This one is just like the original. It has the same essential qualities and features of the original."

This challenges our culture's current view of personal authenticity. In this cultural way of thinking, an authentic human being is one who says "I am different from everyone else. I am myself." By contrast, a truly authentic person is the one who says, "I am a unique expression of all the essential qualities and features of the One in whose image I was made."

John Wesley taught that conversion restores us to our true authenticity because it restores us to the image of God in which we were created. This reality brings a deep inner peace, a rightness about our being. This kind of authenticity drives out fear and self-doubt. We enter into a freedom of being that is not possible in any other way.

Because of this powerful restoration, we are free to interact with others in new ways that are marked by love, respect, patience, kindness, good humor, and joy.

Despite our protestations to the contrary, we are never truly ourselves until we have been restored to the likeness of the One who created us. This is exactly what God does for us when we experience full, free, soul-changing transformation.

This kind of Christian is a marvel to have in the workplace. Few character traits provide a stronger and more attractive foundation for one's life work than the genuineness, trustworthiness, and reliability that come from this deep well-being of soul.

But is this possible?

Chris Foley is an example of a Christian in the Wesleyan tradition who lives out this kind of authenticity in one of the world's most challenging work arenas, the arena of politics.

> Catch on fire with enthusiasm and people will come for miles to watch you burn.
>
> John Wesley

The Public Servant

Chris Foley of Australia has been happily married to his lovely wife, Glenys, for twenty-nine years. They are the parents of six children. But Chris has also been an accountant, private pilot, and television and radio personality, not to mention an award-winning music artist, audio engineer, and black belt Ju-Jitsu instructor. He is also a senior pastor. And did I mention he has been a member of Parliament?

He laughed and said, "I liken the Christian life for me as a rodeo ride. It's been this one bucking-bronco ride of excitement!"

Chris derives the most satisfaction in just helping ordinary people with extraordinary problems; being a pastor and parliamentarian both offer opportunities. Elected in 2003, he served as the independent state member for Maryborough in the Queensland Parliament for nine years. "It was a dual role in that I would make legislation as well as look after the people in my electorate, but in the meantime I also had a very pastoral role in the Parliament." As an independent he was not seen as a threat to anyone, so people of all sides would ask him to help with problems. "When you think about it, it is not too dissimilar from being a pastor," he reflected.

He fought hard for traditional Christian values in the 2012 election, but due to an extraordinary political swing lost his seat by a fraction of a percent. Chris said he discovered how people really viewed him when reading what they wrote to the newspapers. "They talked about integrity, honesty, and behaving in a dignified manner, which is pretty rare in politics, so that was really satisfying. No one talked about job performance because they knew I worked very hard. But it was satisfying to have lived my life as a pastor in a very high profile public life and have people talk about character traits more than job performance."

Chris and Glenys planted Grace Community Church twelve years ago. "One of the features of our church is that because we are a church full of marginalized people, it cannot afford a pastor," he said. Chris has always been a bi-vocational pastor and earned his own money. "It's allowed me a freedom to be absolutely real in every way," he said. He spends the little money the church pays him and way more on ministry opportunities with people in need. "All of my life wherever God has led he has provided," he assured.

"I absolutely loved being in Parliament. I was honored and privileged to do that. In Scripture, Jesus calls us to be salt and light, not just salt and light in our churches—he calls us to be salt and light in our communities."

John Wesley was concerned with the welfare of those in need and encouraged taking risks to minister to everyone. Helping in places of greatest need is an opportunity to make the greatest impact for a believer's mission of reconciling the world to the Father.

"I think if you're really in the center of the will of God, it's like just hang on for a bumpy ride! I've loved every minute of what I'm doing. I say to the people in my church, 'Just trust God and step out; take a few risks, you don't need to have everything safe.' Where God leads he will provide. We've been living proof of that."

Reflection Questions

1. When were you last fooled by thinking something was real when it wasn't?

2. Think about when and how you knew that Jesus is real.

3. What will you do to be authentic?

For Further Reading

Runyon, Theodore. *The New Creation: John Wesley's Theology Today.* Nashville: Abingdon, 1998.

———. "The New Creation: A Wesleyan Distinctive." *Wesleyan Theological Journal* 31, no. 2 (1996): 5–19. http://wesley.nnu.edu/fileadmin/imported_site/wesleyjournal/1996-wtj-31-2.pdf.

Wesley, John. "The Image of God." Genesis 1:27 (sermon, n.p., 1730). *John Wesley's Sermons: An Anthology*, edited by Albert C. Outler and Richard P. Heitzenrater, 14–21. Nashville: Abingdon, 1991.

Wesley, John. "The One Thing Needful." Luke 10:42 (sermon, St. Mary's, Oxford, England; Boston, New England; London, England, et al., 1734–38). In *John Wesley's Sermons: An Anthology*, edited by Albert C. Outler and Richard P. Heitzenrater, 34–38. Nashville: Abingdon, 1991.

What God Has Called Us to Do | PART | 4

Do all the good you can, in all the ways you can,
to all the souls you can, in every place you can,
at all the times you can, with all the zeal you can,
as long as ever you can.

Attributed to John Wesley

Christians whose discipleship is shaped by the truths that gave birth to the great Wesleyan movement pursue their work as particular kinds of people. Christians discipled in the truths of the Wesleyan heritage go to work as people of assurance, people of integrity, and people of authenticity.

Jesus used the metaphors of salt and light to describe the way his followers would permeate and change the world around them. When people of assurance, integrity, and authenticity enter the workplaces of the world, by their very presence they change those places for the better.

But the great Wesleyan movement was not just a movement centered on a message of personal transformation. The Wesleyan movement wasn't only interested in knowing who God has called us to be. It grew from strong convictions about what God has called us to do.

One of the amazing facts about the Wesleyan movement is that, over time, it led to dramatic improvements in the lives of those who embraced its message of transformation. But the central message of this movement was never about the pursuit of personal health and wealth. Instead the Wesleyan movement has been animated by convictions about the way that true conversion makes us act in this world. Wesleyans care deeply about what to believe about Jesus Christ. But this movement has always focused its energy on helping its members live out the transformation that has taken place in their hearts.

Christians living in the Wesleyan tradition of faith embody the sentiment of Proverbs 4:23, "Above all else, guard your heart, for it is the wellspring of life."

Wesleyans are indebted to the Church of England that shaped John Wesley's thinking for this defining characteristic of the movement. Recently a member of an Anglican congregation in the United States was asked what his church believed. He responded, "Come and worship with us and you will see."

Sanctification

John Wesley urged those who joined the movement to see that real conversion leads directly and quickly into a focus on sanctification. Conversion naturally creates a passionate desire to become more like Jesus Christ. The process of becoming like Jesus is called sanctification. This is a word that simply means "becoming holy."

John Wesley's personal experiences convinced him beyond all necessary proof that conversion could not come to us through good works. He was just as deeply convinced that we will never become holy—in other words, we will never embody the love and goodness of Jesus Christ—unless we embrace the work that God has called us to do in this world.

Anyone who has experienced real conversion naturally wants to be in relationship with the One who has saved them. As we walk in relationship with that Person we find Someone who embodies perfect assurance, integrity, and authenticity. In time, as we embrace the task of living this out in the good works to which God calls us, we begin to embody (even if imperfectly) the love and goodness of Jesus.

John Wesley was convinced that doing the good work God has called us to do in this world is inextricably connected to the process of becoming holy. He once put it like this.

> I am convinced of this, and continually maintain this as the truth of God. I am convinced that there is a repentance that follows from, as well as a repentance that precedes justification.
>
> Everyone who is justified is required to be zealous of good works. In fact, this is so necessary that if a person willingly neglects the good works that follow from justification, that person cannot expect to be sanctified. That person cannot grow in grace, in the image of God, in the mind which was in Christ Jesus. That person will not be able even to retain the grace he or she has received, or be able to continue very far in faith, and in the favor of God.
>
> What, then, is the inference we must draw from this?
>
> Why, that both repentance and the practice of all good works—works of piety as well as works of mercy—are, in some sense, necessary to sanctification. ("The Scripture Way of Salvation," III.5)

Further, this good work accomplishes two purposes at once. While God uses this to lead us deeper in the experience of becoming good and wise and godly, God also uses our work to make the world a better place.

The good work to which God calls us makes us better people. At the same time the good work to which God calls us makes the world a better place.

A Framework for Growth

Part of the genius of John and Charles Wesley was that they presented a pathway for personal and spiritual growth that ordinary people could understand and embrace. They laid out a simple but compelling framework for the behavioral transformation that conversion was meant to accomplish. They put in place durable, detailed, and replicable organizational structures that gave people both accountability and assistance in their journey toward wholeness. They provided incredibly rich educational resources to fuel the work of teaching and accountability. They continued to provide detailed and compelling teaching about what it meant to live out the Wesleyan vision of salvation and sanctification.

John and Charles Wesley provided multiple nurturing communities for the members of the movement. First, they encouraged members to continue attending their local parish church. Second, they set up what they called Methodist societies throughout England. These meetings created a community whose members shared new music, testimonies, and teaching. Third, they created "class meetings," which were accountability groups of twelve people arranged in local geographic areas. Fourth, they created "bands." Bands were groups of three to four people arranged according to sex and marital status that came together to accomplish specific things.

The Wesleys encouraged regular meetings. About once a month the Methodist societies gathered for a time of fellowship and testimony. This meeting was called a love feast.

A second monthly service was called the watch night service. This one provided a time of reflection where members would open their hearts to receive correction for sin and recommit themselves to obedience.

Why did John Wesley create so many groups and promote so many special meetings? Each of these meetings provided opportunities for the members of the community to encourage each other and to hold each other accountable. These provided new structures for relationships in a society in which the old social structures were disappearing.

One of the natural effects of this organization was to provide many opportunities for leadership development. Each of these groups required leadership. So they provided a natural way for people to develop the skills of leadership. Also, because of the nature of these groups, they became the recruitment and training mechanism for many female leaders who would never have been given a chance in the formal church structures of the day.

One of the Wesleys' key beliefs was that conversion was offered to all people. This gave them an optimism about people that caused them to create systems that would invite everyone into community. They tried to provide help to everyone who wanted to experience the life transformation that conversion promised. They wanted to help everyone experience the fulfillment that came from serving others in love. (For more on this, see Randy L. Maddox, *Responsible Grace*, 211.)

Three Commitments

Anyone could attend the Society whether they were friend, foe, agnostic, or merely wanted to find out what this commotion was all about. But when they became members, they were asked to do so only if they wished to enter a new level of accountability and dedication to personal growth. When they joined they had to commit themselves to a simple three-part framework for this growth.

First, they had to agree to do no harm by avoiding evil of every kind.

In the context of eighteenth-century England, doing no harm included personal disciplines like not taking the Lord's name in vain, keeping the Sabbath, avoiding drunkenness, not fighting, refraining from taking fellow Christians to court, and refusing to return evil for evil.

Further, it is interesting to note that the Wesleys were not simply private moralists. John Wesley was fully engaged in intellectual and public life, was on personal terms with the nobility, and regularly engaged politicians and business people. So he extended the principle of doing no harm to address evils that were associated with these public arenas. He admonished business owners to refuse to engage in usury, or to borrow without the probability of paying back. He warned customers not to take goods without the probability of paying for them.

Second, they had to agree to do works of mercy according to their means, as often as they could, for as many as they could.

John Wesley was quite specific about what he meant when he called the people of the movement to be merciful. In the England of Wesley's day, there was no social safety net provided by the government. The Industrial Revolution with its mass migration to the city and radically changing circumstances was destroying the traditional community-based values and social networks that had cared for people who fell on hard times.

So the Wesleys called the members of the movement to commit themselves to give food to the hungry, clothing to those who had little, visitation and caregiving to those who were sick and to those who were imprisoned. In general, the Wesleyan movement came to be known for its commitment to help those who were struggling.

Third, they had to agree to make use of what they called the ordinances of God.

The ordinances of God were services of public worship, public and private reading of the Bible, taking the Lord's Supper, praying, and fasting. The members of the Methodist societies were called to commit themselves to regular interaction with the intellectual, spiritual, and emotional resources that fueled their transformation as people.

Further, commitment to the ordinances of God ensured that they would stay plugged into small local communities of Christians intent on pursuing the same journey of development. They would not grow in isolation, nor would they serve alone.

These three commitments were all that was required of those who wished to formally join the Wesleyan movement. There was a particular genius in this on several levels. It was easy to join. Joining the movement didn't require agreement with elaborate and controversial doctrinal statements. Joining didn't require taking any particular position on the many hotly contested social issues of the day. Joining wasn't associated with any particular political party. Joining wasn't associated with any socioeconomic status. Wealthy and poor people alike committed themselves to this program of personal and spiritual growth.

But joining was not for the faint of heart. The commitments were demanding. There was no place to hide if you didn't follow through. Joining meant committing yourself to real behavioral changes that were not easy and that would be clearly obvious to everyone else in the society. Above all, joining meant belonging to a community of others committed to this same agenda of personal growth and outward facing service to others outside the community. (Information in this section is drawn from John Wesley, "The Nature, Design, and General Rules of the United Societies" [1743].)

Discipleship and the Transformation of Social Systems

The genius of the Wesleys was that through the combination of their message of conversion and these frameworks for personal growth, members of the movement were led to embrace two transforming discipleship challenges.

The first discipleship challenge that Wesleyans embrace is to become holy people. Our hearts come to belong to Jesus Christ without reservation. Our lives come to reflect the orienting presence of Christ and embody the way of love, joy, peace, patience, kindness, goodness, faithfulness, gentleness, and self-control (Gal. 5:22–23). The great Wesleyan movement, at its root, was a movement of people who experienced the life-transforming happiness of becoming holy. Far from being a people of drudgery and legalism, their pursuit of holiness made the Wesleyans a community of happiness, hope, and well-being. This is the first of our whole-life discipleship challenges.

The second discipleship challenge that John Wesley called the Wesleyan movement to embrace is that our homes, the communities in which our homes are situated, and the society comprised of our communities should become holy. Wesleyans do not only embrace the personal discipleship challenge of becoming holy individuals. John Wesley called the great movement that grew from his ministry to embrace the challenge of ensuring that our communities, too, come to reflect the values, the structures, and the practices that make them places of grace, hope, happiness, optimism, fairness, discipline, and well-being.

As Wesleyans, some of us live in societies where we are not free to shape them overtly according to the good news and the good sense of Jesus Christ. We cannot openly offer the principles of community peace and well-being that are embedded in the Bible. Others of us enjoy the great blessing of political freedom not only to give our influence to shape our societies in this way, but to do so overtly as a holy people, the people of Jesus Christ.

Still, all of us, when we are most faithful to and most aware of our Wesleyan heritage, will realize that we are called to both of these discipleship challenges. We are called to become holy people. We are called to use our influence to see that our communities and our societies become holy societies.

But what does this really mean? Does this mean that we are called to impose our vision of a holy lifestyle on our neighbors?

Well, in terms of the broad moral challenges of community life, it would certainly mean that we use our influence to shape communities that honor principles of fairness and justice as well as compassion and mercy.

But Wesley's example is fascinating and instructive on this score. It is well-known that while Wesley's personal surroundings were well-ordered and of good quality, he himself was deeply committed to living a plain and unostentatious life. Yet Wesley's legacy was not one of seeking to impose plain lifestyle laws on English society. Instead, what it meant for Wesley to engage with his society to make it a more holy place can be summarized in challenges he issued.

First, he challenged the people of the Wesleyan movement to care for those who were most vulnerable in their communities, those in most danger, those whose lives were in the most danger of being destroyed both by their personal failures and by the broader forces at work in the society.

Second, he challenged the people who could shape the structures and systems of society to do so in ways that promoted such values as freedom, access, fairness, and dignity for all. He called for laws that promoted the well-being of the whole of English society.

Third, he challenged the Wesleyans themselves to be people of industry, creativity, discipline, and thrift. And then, when these practices began to pay off with accumulated wealth (as they will almost always do), he challenged the Wesleyans to use their wealth to ensure the well-being of others, not simply to collect their wealth into great personal estates.

In the great John Wesley movement of eighteenth-century England, the discipleship challenge of making communities holy places was not primarily about imposing Wesley's brand of religious belief, or Wesley's convictions about a holy lifestyle, on everyone else. It was about ensuring that the society was ordered in such a way that everyone had the chance to life lives characterized by dignity, happiness, hope, grace, and fairness. He lived this out by giving away his own considerable wealth to those in need. He also lived this out by challenging the people in power to pass laws that shaped the politics and the economy of the day according to principles of fairness, access, and dignity for all.

To put it succinctly, the John Wesley vision of whole-life discipleship requires two elements. One is to create a community framework that embodies biblical principles of peace, fairness, and hope for all. The other is to allow God to make us holy people so that we will use that fairness to create lives of goodness and happiness.

Lifestyles don't change because of legislation. Legislation, by itself, will not make a community holy. If lifestyles change, they change because our hearts change. Our hearts change when we truly encounter Jesus Christ, and embrace a life of loving, meaningful service to others.

This is the genius of the Wesleyan movement—Wesley's optimism about the possibility of true personal holiness and his conviction that both forms of discipleship, the discipleship of personal life and of community life, are necessary for us to become fully transformed in the image of God.

So let's explore just a bit further what it might mean to practice community discipleship. To use our common language today, this would mean we seek to shape the legal, political, and economic systems of our day so that they embody biblical principles. Positively, the economy is the social system through which people organize their work and dispose of its fruits. Some of its main characteristics include employment and pay, property ownership, exchange, business, and investment. When followers of Jesus think about economics, we are interested in the extraction of economic wisdom and virtue from Scripture and from our specific theological traditions. Economic wisdom can be extracted from biblical passages and stories that extend across the following areas: debt, giving, saving, evil uses of money, the poor, and riches. Some, but by no means all, of the corresponding economic virtues and vices can be seen in the following list: honesty/integrity, prudence, shrewdness, frugality/thrift, stewardship, contentment, coveting, greed, idolatry, partiality, industriousness, and so on.

These concepts are all deeply embedded in the DNA of our Wesleyan heritage. John Wesley encouraged us to think of our discipleship task as including our personal orientation to virtues like these, but also our community's orientation to virtues like these.

It may be possible, for example, to legislate thrift. But if we want a community where thrift becomes a way of life, we need two things. We need a legal, political, and economic system that allows and rewards thrift. And we need a people whose hearts are motivated to pursue thrift. And if we want a holy community, we must become people whose hearts are motivated to pursue thrift *so that* we can promote the well-being of others, not just through charitable giving, but through the entrepreneurial use of the resources that our thrift produces. And we want a legal, political, and economic system that allows and rewards that kind of action.

This little primer is not the place to explore legal, political, and economic systems. The burden of this primer is simply to point out that discipleship includes both elements—personal holiness and community holiness expressed not as a set of lifestyle laws imposed on all, but as a set of values that helps us shape legal, political, and economic systems so they become places of grace, hope, happiness, optimism, fairness, discipline, and well-being for all.

Some Wesleyan Principles for Good Work

With that broader transformation in view, let us finish off this section with a review of a simple framework of principles that forever shape the way that Wesleyans think about the work that God has called us to do.

First, God has called us to ensure that our work does no harm.

Wesleyans pursue work that does no harm to the environment, to the creation at large, to themselves, or to their neighbors. Our work is motivated by a compassionate spirit, and is itself the expression of our loving service to others.

Second, God has called us to pursue work that meets real human needs.

Wesleyans pursue work that looks for needs and finds creative ways to meet them. Our work, no matter what it is, always seeks to promote personal well-being both for those who serve and those who receive service. Our work creates value and spreads that value as far and wide as possible.

Third, God has called us to anchor our work in healthy communities.

Wesleyans pursue work that promotes community well-being. We see our work itself as one of God's holiest gifts by which we celebrate the magnificent richness of God's creation, and through which we are invited to create communities marked by beauty, creativity, order, justice, and abundance.

Reflection Questions

1. How does the concept of sanctification, or becoming holy, inform your understanding of discipleship?
2. How does God help you to become holy?
3. How does your community of believers help you to grow in faith and godliness?
4. How do the commitments that your community of believers makes to each other compare to the commitments of the Wesleyan societies?
5. How do you live out the Wesleyan principle for good work?

For Further Reading

Maddox, Randy L. *Responsible Grace: John Wesley's Practical Theology.* Nashville: Kingswood Books, 1994.

Wesley, John. "The Nature, Design, and General Rules of the United Societies (1743)." In *The Methodist Societies: History, Nature, and Design.* Edited by Rupert E. Davis. Vol. 9 of *The Bicentennial Edition of the Works of John Wesley*, 68–73. Nashville: Abingdon, 1989.

Work That Promotes Personal Well-Being
4

> Give me one hundred preachers who
> fear nothing but sin and desire nothing
> but God, and I care not a straw whether
> they be clergymen or laymen, such alone
> will shake the gates of hell and set up
> the kingdom of heaven upon earth.
>
> **John Wesley**

One of the most powerful factors that shaped the great Wesleyan movement was John Wesley's passionate engagement with the crushing unmet needs of common people in eighteenth-century England.

It was a time of emerging promise intellectually, technologically, and economically. For those with the mind and will to see and embrace innovation, a new dawn of possibility was opening on the horizon. Within a hundred years unbelievable wealth would be created. Great new vistas of knowledge would be opened. The world was literally opening up before those who wished to explore.

But at the same moment, these great shifts of knowledge, technology, politics, and economics created a troubling by-product.

The morals that had anchored English society were being weakened by changing circumstances. The stable social structures that gave people identity and security were coming undone. The result was human wreckage that no one quite had the will or the knowledge to address. Instead of accepting this as the necessary consequence of progress, John Wesley called the people of his movement to reach out to those who were becoming the unfortunate unintended consequences of history's forward march.

The Wesleyans firmly believed that all people matter to God. They were convinced that all of society should be restored to the image of God. The Wesleys were inspired in their pursuit of holistic well-being for all people by the phrase in the Lord's Prayer that says, "Thy will be done on earth as it is in heaven." So they set out to evaluate the health of their society and then to devise and prescribe solutions that they believed would make earth a little more like heaven, or at least like the earth God might have intended.

This is the legacy that Wesleyans embrace today and that lays down a pattern for us as we embrace a full-orbed discipleship of work. John Wesley specifically called those who had come to be deeply, thoroughly, and gloriously saved to give their lives to work that would make the world a better place for individual people as well as whole communities.

They called Wesleyans to embrace both the beauty and the ugliness of the world. The people of the Wesleyan movement were called to engage with both the opportunities and the brokenness they saw around them. They could neither ignore, nor accept as inevitable, the hurt and brokenness in their world.

Our Wesleyan heritage calls us to ensure that our work promotes personal well-being, and work that promotes community well-being. A Wesleyan discipleship of work causes us to ask, how can both the content and the form of our work help to restore the world in the image of God?

Well-Being in the Real-World Workplace

When we embrace this question today, we must immediately come to terms with a world of work that is in some ways very different from Wesley's eighteenth-century England. Advances in scientific and engineering knowledge, technology, communication, and transportation have created a world of work that would be scarcely recognizable to John and Charles Wesley.

Still, if the Wesleys were here now, they would still be asking questions like these:

- ⟡ How can we use our great knowledge and skill to create the most wealth for the most people?

- ⟡ As we pursue great advances in the world of work who is getting left behind?

- ⟡ What are the unintended consequences of our great advances in industry and commerce?

- ⟡ Who might be getting hurt as we pursue our great opportunities for growth?

These were the questions the Wesleyan movement addressed in the eighteenth-century. We must believe that John Wesley would ask the same questions today. Since he is not here, our Wesleyan discipleship of work must drive us to do the asking.

Our Wesleyan heritage embraces the opportunities of our time. But it forces us to pursue opportunity in ways that protect the personal well-being of those who are most vulnerable to the unintended consequences of progress. This comes right down to the way in which we engage opportunities in our personal workplace. Our whole-life discipleship of work pushes us to shape our own workplace in such a way as to promote our own well-being and the well-being of our co-workers.

It certainly pushes those of us in management and leadership positions to ensure that in our pursuit of opportunity and abundance, we remember that our first obligation is to promote the well-being of those who share our work. It is easy for us to embrace the Wesleyan admonition to earn all we can. It is not always so easy as workers and as leaders to embrace the equally Wesleyan admonition to only do so in ways that do no harm and that promote the well-being of all who are involved in our enterprises.

Some have called this a "covenant relationship" with our work. This kind of relationship, so naturally Wesleyan in its thinking, is contrasted with the "transactional relationship" that so typically prevails in the world of work. As we pursue this covenant relationship we must come to terms with the fact that our workplaces are all too often places of opposition and dysfunction. As individual workers, and as those who manage the work of others, we must ask ourselves questions such as these:

- ✧ How can I thrive in a workplace that is unhealthy?
- ✧ How can I be an agent of redemption when work becomes a curse?
- ✧ How can I create a workplace that is healthy?
- ✧ How can I be an agent of grace so that the workplace becomes a blessing?

It is good to remind ourselves of life in the real-world workplace.

A Story from the Real-World Workplace

Newly divorced, with two children, and needing a steady paycheck, Jenny took work at a small nonprofit organization as the public relations and marketing director.

"I knew going in that the work situation wasn't ideal," said Jenny. "It was a small, underfunded organization with crummy computer equipment and a small staff. Everyone was overextended in one way or another."

On her first day of work Jenny began to realize the challenges she would face in maintaining personal well-being in a workplace that could be quite unhealthy. "I started on the same day as another woman, whose job involved outdoor maintenance. She showed up to work wearing khaki pants and a button-down shirt—her attempt to dress appropriately for an outdoors job taking care of thousands of trees in our city. She was criticized and nearly sent home to change." The supervisor wanted to know why the new tree services manager wasn't wearing a skirt and pantyhose to work.

Jenny quickly learned about the unstable emotional terrain of her new work. "The job was more about appeasing the boss and stabilizing her very unstable moods than it was about actually doing your job," explained Jenny. And in addition, the boss had what Jenny calls "ever-shifting and unrealistic expectations and requirements."

The organization struggled to keep its doors open because so much time, attention, and energy that could have gone toward helping the organization excel was spent instead on managing internal conflicts. Jenny tried as best she could to manage the negative toll her job took on her work and personal life, but ultimately she was left no option but to quit.

Unfortunately, Jenny's story is not as rare as we would hope. A 2011 poll done by Harris Interactive for the American Psychological Association found that "36 percent of workers report ongoing work stress, most of which is related to negative or outright unhealthy management practices." Nearly half of those workers reported that the presence of "heavy workload, long hours and unrealistic expectations" were among the sources of emotional distress. The poll goes on to show that nearly half of the disgruntled employees don't feel valued at work, and that one-third intend to look for another job before the year is out. (See Douglas La-Bier, "The Lowdown on Abusive Bosses and the Unhealthy Work-place—Part 1." *Psychology Today*, June 25, 2011.)

Unfortunately, this is all too often the reality of the real-world workplace for many people. Our Wesleyan discipleship of work calls for us as individual workers to pursue well-being at work. It calls for us as managers and those serving in leadership to do all we can to promote personal well-being at work.

So, what do we do when work becomes a curse? What do we do when we find ourselves suffering at the hands of the vocation to which we feel called?

Beyond a certain level of providing a living wage and treating workers fairly given the proceeds of an enterprise, personal well-being at work is not usually promoted by giving people things or by making their work easier. Personal well-being at work comes from ensuring that our workplace honors deeper principles. Let's examine some Wesleyan principles that guide us at this point.

Work and Inner Happiness

John Wesley was deeply aware of the reality that life's circum-stances are all too often unpleasant and unhappy. The Wesleyan revival took place mostly among people for whom life wasn't easy. Their work was not pleasant. It didn't pay well. They lived in tenu-ous circumstances.

In fact, many of the world's people go to work every day in jobs that are tedious, menial, and dangerous. We cannot always ar-range our lives so that our jobs are fulfilling and challenging. Some-times our best opportunities still leave a lot to be desired. And sometimes we go through seasons when our work takes every-thing we have to give, and then some.

Wesleyan whole-life discipleship brought to life this work-transforming reality. The deep personal transformation that comes from loving Jesus with all our hearts, lived out in loving fellowship with a small group of fellow believers, brings into play in our work situations a powerful resource of inner happiness, despite the drudgery and burden that many people in the eighteenth century were enduring with social and economic conditions such as they were.

One especially important effect of Wesley's teaching and the corresponding revival in England was the sense of Christian joy and inner happiness that resulted from people's experience of conversion and sanctification which in turn set them free to approach the toil and frustration of their work in a new way. Thus Wesley's belief was that Christian happiness can be experienced in the midst of one's job and be a part of the larger "work" of experiencing holiness of heart and life.

When there is nothing beyond our work, or in our work, that stirs the deepest feelings of fulfillment, meaning, and well-being, work can grind our spirits and our bodies into submission. By all means, when we have the capacity to create good work for others, we should do it. That subject has its own chapter in this book (see chap. 5). When we can arrange to engage in work that challenges us, that expresses our sense of calling, and takes advantage of our gifts, we should do it.

But sometimes, our jobs can be little more than a way to earn the living that keeps body and soul together for another day, that allows us to care for our family. When we pass through these seasons, our heritage calls us to go deep into the soul of our faith, to find the seeds of inner happiness planted in our hearts by the presence of God's Spirit, and to engage the fellowship of our fellow Christians.

One of the miracles of whole-life discipleship is that, where it has taken root in this world, it has not immediately upended buckets of money on people. It has not suddenly given privilege and power to those who lacked it. Instead, the genius of the Wesleyan movement is that it gave people who lacked money, who had no power, who enjoyed the least prestige—it gave these very people an inner dignity and an unquenchable happiness that slowly, steadily, and surely transformed their lives, and through them, transformed the societies in which they lived. This is where well-being at work begins.

Wesleyan Principles That Promote Personal Well-Being at Work

John Wesley did not write much that spoke directly about the workplace. But his ministry did embody principles that we can identify and apply in this context. His messages contain principles that can guide us as we pursue personal well-being in our work.

First, we are called to create workplaces that promote the well-being of both body and soul.

In eighteenth-century England few people had the benefit of much formal education, and fewer still had the benefit of gaining access to medical care. Usually, the most highly educated person in a village would be the clergyman. Consequently, Oxford University included coursework that prepared pastors to give basic medical advice. This was true of John Wesley, and it led to an interesting and instructive part of his ministry.

One of John Wesley's most widely distributed books was a little volume called *Primitive Physick*. True to his principles, as Wesley traveled around England, deeply in tune with the needs of common people, he realized that very few of them had any access to health care. So he went through the texts to which he had access and compiled this little manual for basic medical advice, then ensured that every Methodist society had at least one copy, and that the Methodist preachers had access to it.

By the standards of modern medicine, Wesley's *Primitive Physick* is "primitive" to be sure. But by the standards of the day, it represented the best available advice. What's most important for us, however, is that it represented a genuine attempt to meet the needs of the people he met through his ministries. Not only did John Wesley try to assure that the common folk of the day got access to medical advice, he also took the trouble to set up apothecary shops so that they could buy the best available treatments of the day at the affordable prices.

Here was the great preacher, John Wesley, doing some very interesting things. He was seeking to ensure the holistic well-being of his neighbors by finding innovative ways to meet an obvious need that others ignored. He was doing so using entrepreneurial business practices that addressed both physical and spiritual dimensions of human life. And he did this by paying special attention to the people on the margins of society. This is just about as Wesleyan a train of events as is possible to imagine.

Most importantly, this work represented a principle that was deeply rooted in the Christian faith—the principle that we are called to do work that cares for the well-being of both body and soul. This great principle became, and remains, one of the core defining characteristics of a Wesleyan discipleship of work.

Noted Wesley studies scholar and professor Randy Maddox articulates the core principle like this:

> Wesley tells us not to make sharp distinctions between caring for your soul and for your body. To care for your body is a spiritual duty. He's deeply aware of the way spiritual things can impact us physically and physical things spiritually. At a personal level, Wesley tells us to be more integrated persons,

and then secondly he is asking us to look at how we support our communities and provide outreach to others. He clearly wants us to reach out not just to care for souls but to care for bodies. (Randy Maddox, "The Holistic Vision of John Wesley," interview by John Shorb, *Church Health Reader*, October 25, 2010)

This is the principle that we must honor in our discipleship of work. When we approach our own work, and when we shape our workplaces, we must do so with this principle in mind. We are called to create workplaces that care for the whole person.

This principle deeply rooted in the Wesleyan movement helped to give birth to one of England's most venerable and visible retail companies—Boots Chemists. Boots Chemist shops are friendly and have ubiquitous presence on virtually every high-street shopping area in British towns of any size. International travelers now see Boots Chemist shops in airports around the world. Perhaps few know that this great international company owes its roots to Jesse Boot's upbringing in the eighteenth-century Wesleyan movement, and the specific ideas he took from John Wesley's *Primitive Physick*.

Let's hear the story in the words of the Boots company as it is told in an article on the NgTrader website titled "The History of Boots the Chemist—Nottingham."

As a child, Jesse Boot accompanied his father into the woods, identifying plants for his herbal remedies. Jesse was only ten years old when his father died. He left school at thirteen and started to help his mother, Mary, full-time in their little shop, which sold soap, soda, camomile, senna, household necessities and simple herbal remedies. In any spare time he had, Jesse would learn all he could about pharmacy.

In 1877, Jesse took control of the chemist's shop in Goose Gate, selling "Drugs and Proprietary Articles at Reduced Prices," and introduced lines such as black lead and candles. He had worked out how he could undercut the monopoly of the "proper" chemists who practised a price-fixing policy: he had to raise his sales to £20 a week in order to buy in large quantities and sell at low prices. He advertised in the Nottingham Daily Express informing readers of the 128 items he stocked from Allen's Hair Restorer to Woodhouse's Rheumatic Elixir, emphasizing their reduced prices. His tactics provoked violent opposition from other chemists. Within the first month his takings had risen to £40 per week.

Jesse Boot's aim was to attract working-class people who could now afford a few of the things he had to offer and for their benefit he also created some special offers such as soft soap at 41/2d for 2lb, when other shops were selling it at 4d a 1lb. On such occasions, he would have a bell-ringer touring the streets of Nottingham which brought customers flocking to his shop. *His hard work and concern for the poor came from his ardent Methodist upbringing and adherence to the John Wesley Primitive Physic for his folk medicine. Later he renamed his shop "The People's Store."* (emphasis added)

Second, we are called to create workplaces that meet basic human needs with fairness and compassion.

Another principle that John Wesley raised to prominence within the Wesleyan movement was a passionate commitment to ensure that people's basic human needs were met. He did this through his own legendary charitable giving. He firmly believed that every pound or dollar not necessary for our own care and the care of our families, and not needed for the care of our enterprises, was intended to be turned to the use of others whose needs remained unmet or to support enterprises and ministries whose operations needed to be funded.

One of John Wesley's most poignant expressions of this constant focus on the call to ensure that people's basic human needs were met comes in his sermon entitled "Heaviness through Manifold Temptations."

> Has poverty nothing worse in it than this, that it makes men liable to be laughed at? Is not want of food something worse than the possibility of ridicule?
>
> God pronounced it as a curse upon man that he should earn his food by the sweat of his brow. But how many are there in this Christian country that toil, and labor, and sweat, and still are not able to earn their food, but struggle with weariness and hunger together?
>
> Is this not made worse when, after a hard day's labor, he comes back to a poor, cold, dirty, uncomfortable lodging, to find there not even the food which is needful to repair his wasted strength?
>
> You that live at ease on this earth, that want nothing, is it not a worse effect to seek bread day by day and find none than to suffer ridicule?
>
> Were it not that he is restrained by an unseen hand, surely the one who suffers from want of food would soon curse God and die. O want of bread! Want of bread! Who can tell what this means, unless he has felt this want himself?
>
> I am astonished that this great need creates no more than a sense of "heaviness" among those who believe. (III.3)

One cannot spend any time at all with John Wesley without being affected by this passionate, unwavering commitment to know the real needs of real people, and to respond by finding every conceivable means to meet these needs.

Wesley's movement challenged the normal human responses to such needs. It is normal to turn our eyes away from such needs. It is normal to explain away such needs. It is normal to assume that needy people will help themselves or be helped by others. It is normal to engage ourselves in all manner of trivial and noble pursuits in the hope that somehow the needs of others will be met. It is normal to pray for God to meet the needs of those whose basic needs go unmet.

Wesley could not do any of these things. Something in his spiritual DNA, kept calling him back to a sense of personal responsibility. He did everything he could, and he called the members of the movement to ensure that every resource, every charitable and entrepreneurial means, would be used to be sure that the basic needs of every human being would be met.

How does this principle work itself out in the real-world workplace? We do not have space here to unpack the application of this principle. But we can give an example.

An overriding truth runs through the movement—Wesley saw every human being as a creature created in the image of God, and thus a person worthy of being treated with dignity. This deep commitment to treat even the "least" of society with dignity encouraged those very people to treat themselves, their families, and their surroundings with greater responsibility. This in turn led to the creation of great value.

Thus, it might be considered an axiom growing from the movement, that those organizations, those governments, those societies, and those economies that treat people with dignity and expect and reward personal responsibility will waste fewer resources on managing toxicity and will enjoy the benefit of greater rewards. Of course, it almost goes without saying that every workplace that embraces this biblical principle would do its best to provide healthy wage and working conditions. But basic human needs go beyond this. So let's look at a set of examples of how one would use this principle to shape an approach to work that promotes personal well-being.

Those who study today's real-world workplace say that workplace stress has become a major problem eroding both the quality of work and life. In a 1990 study titled "Prevention of Work-Related

Psychological Disorders," published in the *American Psychologist*, Steven L. Sauter and his colleagues reviewed the work-stress literature and identified six common causes for work stress: (1) workload and work pace, (2) role stressors, (3) career concerns, (4) work scheduling, (5) job content and control, and (6) interpersonal relationships. Let's see how a few or so of these represent basic human needs that would be addressed by our whole-life approach to the discipleship of work.

Workload and Work Pace

Americans are working more than ever before. Statistics from the National Institute of Occupational Safety and Health in 2002 showed that the average work year for working couples had gone up by nearly seven hundred hours in the previous two decades. In their article, "Building Healthy Workplaces: What We Know So Far," published in the *Canadian Journal of Behavioural Science*, Kevin Kelloway and Arla Day show the negative impact of being overworked. "The strains associated with being overworked have been found to be uniformly negative across behavioural, psychological, and physiological outcome domains" (224). In other words, working too hard for too long hurts us in every way. A Wesleyan discipleship of work that took this fact seriously would make us as individual workers, and as workplace leaders, seek God's guidance to create a healthy balance so our physical health, our family relationships, and our spiritual life are not damaged by overwork.

Role Stressors

Another way in which our basic human needs go unmet is when we are unable to reconcile two or more conflicting role demands in the workplace. This happens, for example, if we are asked to carry out incompatible tasks by different supervisors or bosses. It happens when we are left consistently unsure about what is expected of us in our jobs. Finally, we experience role stress when we face "inter-role conflict," such as work-family demands, when our jobs interfere with our roles as parent or spouse, or vice versa. Following the principles of our Wesleyan discipleship, as people of assurance and integrity, we need to seek honest clarification and guard the boundaries of our lives and the lives of others.

Career Concerns

Constantly having to worry about our job security, the possibility of downsizing (or becoming redundant), layoffs, or being fired can create a substantial amount of stress in the real-world workplace today. Job security is not an unreasonable concern. And if we are not worried about losing our jobs, we may be harboring stress around career development. Further, studies show that for many, workplace safety or the lack thereof, creates a significant amount of stress.

When our spiritual anchors are set deeply in the assurance of God's calling and presence, we are not as vulnerable to these kinds of stresses. But this does not mean that we should not address these basic human needs in our workplaces. It is sometimes possible for workplace leaders to use uncertainty about the future as a workplace motivator.

Early in my career when I attempted to share a concern about our workplace with the owner of the company, he quickly told me that he could hire ten other people to do my job; he simply was not interested in hearing what I had to share. Faithfulness to a Wesleyan discipleship of work will not lead to perfect agreement between workers, and between workers and workplace leaders. But it will lead to a desire to hear and meet workplace needs as much as possible, and in doing this, will ultimately lead to more healthy and productive workplaces.

Interpersonal Relationships

Above all these other stressors, interpersonal conflict can be the most devastating to our personal well-being. Kelloway and Day note that interpersonal relationships can cause stress in the workplace in one of two ways: "1) a lack of coworker and supervisory support; and 2) the presence of violence and aggression" (226). Not having the support of our colleagues can take our feet out from under us. Conversely, a vast body of research shows that having strong social support in our workplace can actually buffer the negative effects of these other work-related stressors.

It's remarkable how much power we hold as individuals to mark the course of our colleagues' days. A Wesleyan discipleship of work calls us to conduct ourselves at work in ways that give honor and respect to our co-workers, those we serve, and those who are in places of leadership. This would be a mutual pursuit to make the workplace a safe place—not a place without conflict or disagreement—but a place in which disagreement and differences are treated with respect and used to positive effect.

Third, we are called to create workplaces that embrace the principle of "peacemaking."

A third principle in the Wesleyan discipleship of the workplace rests on a train of thought that is expressed throughout John Wesley's work. Indeed we have touched on it repeatedly throughout this primer. But this train of thought is expressed most succinctly in a famous sermon Wesley preached on Jesus' Sermon on the Mount. Here is the way the logic behind this principle goes.

First, every bit of God's creation has intrinsic worth because it belongs to God and is loved by God. In writing about Jesus' teaching in the Sermon on the Mount, Wesley wrote:

> The lesson which our blessed Lord inculcates here . . . is that God is in all things, and that we are to see the Creator in the face of every creature; that we should use and look upon nothing as separate from God, which indeed is a kind of prac-

tical atheism; but with a true magnificence of thought we should consider heaven and earth and all that is therein as contained by God in the hallow of his hand, who by his intimate presence holds them all in being, who pervades and actuates the whole created frame, and is in a true sense the soul of the universe. ("Upon Our Lord's Sermon on the Mount: Discourse Three," I.11)

When we work with the minerals and the chemicals and the plants of this world, we are not using indiscriminate raw material that has only instrumental value. We are working with the created splendor of God. When we work through the creativity and energy and agency of employees, we are not working with nameless and faceless "labor." We are working with the most majestic of all God's creatures. Everything we touch, everything we create, everything we discharge, everyone we employ, everyone we serve in our work— we are to see the Creator in the face of every single one of these.

We work in the garden of the great creator God. All of our work is a participation in and an expression of God's beauty and purpose. The effect of our work on creation, whether for good or ill, is either to extend or to diminish the majesty of God's creation. There are no innocent bystanders in the world of work. There are no expendable resources. There are no throwaways. God is present in it all. As the apostle Paul puts it, "For from him and through him and to him are all things," and "in him we live and move and have our being" (Rom. 11:36; Acts 17:28).

Second, Wesley was very conscious of another great reality. It would be wonderful if that first reality told the whole story. But it does not. The painful truth is that all of creation has been damaged by the fall. All of creation groans under the curse of sin. Sin has introduced suspicion, selfishness, and destructive conflict into the creation. Sin has put the noble calling of humans to work under the curse of sweat and pain and toil. Our work is carried out on a battlefield where there is a need for peace.

Third, thankfully God is present in his world offering peace, reconciliation, and redemption. God works to restore all of creation to the splendor of the image, and the hopefulness of the promise, for which he created it. To do that, he calls us to the ministry of peacemaking. Here is how John Wesley put this:

> In the full extent of the word a "peacemaker" is one who, as he has opportunity "does good unto all men"; one who being filled with the love of God and of all mankind cannot confine the expressions of that love to his own family, or friends, or acquaintance, or party; no, nor to those who are partakers of like precious faith. A peacemaker steps over all these boundaries so that he may do good to every man; so that he may in some way or other manifest his love to neighbors and strangers, friends and enemies. ("Upon Our Lord's Sermon on the Mount: Discourse Three," II.4)

In a Wesleyan discipleship of work, we see our work itself as an enterprise in peacemaking. We enter the workplace as peacemakers. As leaders of the workplace we are called to be peacemakers.

Peacemakers, according to the principles embodied in the Scripture, are those who find every possible way to do something good for others. The enterprises we undertake are aimed at doing something good in the world. Wesleyan workers are always looking for ways to share God's love at work—not necessarily to "witness" to others, not always to tell others, but to do for others what is in their best interests.

Workplace leaders are always looking for ways to do something good not only for their clients and customers, but also for all those who work in their chain of supply, employment, and distribution. This is a workplace ethic of peacemaking. It is an expression of our calling to do work that promotes personal well-being. Let us take a moment to bring this home with a concrete example.

Unfortunately, the workplace can be a brutal place. A recent survey by the Workplace Bullying Institute (WBI) shows that 35 percent of people have experienced workplace bullying. According to the Institute, workplace bullying is the mistreatment of one or more persons called "the target" by one or more "perpetrators." This mistreatment can take the form of any of the following:

✧ verbal abuse

✧ offensive conduct/behaviors (including nonverbal) which are threatening, humiliating, or intimidating

✧ work interference—sabotage—which prevents work from getting done

In the *Psychology Today* article on abusive bosses mentioned earlier, business psychologist and psychotherapist Douglas LaBier reports that workplace trauma can wound us significantly: "There's even some evidence that psychologically unhealthy management can create a form of post-traumatic stress disorder, like that seen among soldiers returning from combat" ("The Lowdown on Abusive Bosses and the Unhealthy Workplace—Part 1").

Surprisingly, workplace bullying is not like school playground bullying. Unlike the type of bullying that happens during adolescence when the loner or perceived "weakling" gets picked on, workplace bullying is often focused on the strongest and most liked workers. The People Bottomline website reported that "[v]ictims are often selected for unfair treatment because of their abilities and competence and for the perceived threat they pose to the perpetrator's career ambitions."

According to the WBI website, "targets" of workplace bullying exhibit the following characteristics:

✧ Targets are independent.

✧ They are more technically skilled than their bullies.

✧ They are better liked and have more social skills.

✧ They are ethical and honest. They tend to be the whistle-blowers, the workers who refuse to let unethical practices flourish in their work space.

✧ They are nonconfrontative. They tend to take the high-road and refuse to retaliate, which, unfortunately, allows the bully free reign to behave badly.

Whatever the reasons for unhealthy work environments, a wealth of literature says that our work has a profound impact on our mental, physical, and emotional health. Our personal health is intimately connected to the health of our work.

When we embrace the call to work in a way that promotes personal well-being, and when we embrace the principle of peace-making, we must look clearly at our workplace to ask if we see any trace of the trauma of such mistreatment. Though it is hard to address this issue, our commitment to a biblical understanding of work calls us to be peacemakers in a world that all too often settles for such destructive and selfish conflict.

This pursuit is a healthy reward in itself. But such a commitment carries with it another reward that seems self-evident but is sadly too often overlooked. When an organization ensures that everyone within the organization is given the dignity of participating in managing the peace of the organization, fewer resources will have to be spent on managing discord and strife. More focus can be laid on the creation of value for those whom the organization exists to serve.

Thus, when we strive to make our workplaces peaceful, we become "value creators." Value creators are good for organizations because the fundamental reason we work is to produce value for others, and the more value creators any organization has, the more likely it is to thrive among those it seeks to serve.

Fourth, we are called to create workplaces whose ultimate goal is to bring glory to God.

When we consider the fact that we are called to pursue work that promotes personal well-being, we may be tempted to think of our work as something we do for our own personal benefit.

As we have seen, our Wesleyan discipleship of work leads us to pursue the well-being of body and soul, to do work that meets basic human needs, and to do our work as peacemakers in this world— seeking to do good at every turn. By following these principles our work becomes generative and not consuming. We do not simply extract the wealth from the resources of the land and the talents of the people we employ. Our work aims to create and restore.

But ultimately, what is the purpose of work that pursues personal well-being? Well-run organizations have goals. John Wesley asks the powerful question: What is the ultimate goal of a well-run workplace? Is it merely to create wealth? Is it just to create beauty and order out of chaos? Is it to put food on the table for the most people?

Here is Wesley's response—a response that is embedded in the movement he founded.

> "In what spirit do you run your business? Do you run your business in the spirit of the world, or the Spirit of Christ?"
>
> I am afraid thousands of those who are called good Christians do not understand the question. If you act in the Spirit of Christ . . . you do everything in the spirit of sacrifice, giving up your will to the will of God, and continually aiming not at ease, pleasure, or riches; not at anything this short enduring world can give; but merely at the glory of God.
>
> Now can anyone deny that this is the most excellent way of pursuing worldly business? ("The More Excellent Way," III.3)

Who owns our work? Ultimately, God does.

Who owns the resources with which we work? Ultimately, God does.

Whose are the people with whom we work? Ultimately, they are God's chosen and loved people?

Long after we are gone, the product of our work will either disappear into the dim memories of history, or it will endure as a lasting testimony to enduring values and practices. Ultimately, the factor that determines this outcome, will be the choice we made about the spirit in which we offered the treasure of our work.

If we try to own it, it will someday be given to someone else.

If we try to control it, control will someday be passed to someone else.

If we try to hoard the wealth it produces, our treasures will someday be given to someone else to spend.

If we make it about our own ease or reputation or pleasure, these will elude our grasp even on the day of our greatest achievements.

But if we offer our work up as a living sacrifice for God to use in his peacemaking, splendor creating, knowledge unfolding goodness, our work will satisfy our deepest desires, meet our deepest needs, and bear fruit for eternity.

Can this work in real life? It certainly can. Many have proven these principles. Now meet George Jetter, one man who lived out these principles.

> A constant attention to the work which God entrusts us with
> is a mark of solid piety.
>
> John Wesley

The Entrepreneurs

George Jetter's lifelong passion for giving began on an Ohio River cruise while listening to industrial philanthropist R. G. LeTourneau. "He wanted to get into business any way he could!" exclaimed his wife, Esther Jetter.

Like LeTourneau, George wanted to dedicate his business to serving Christ. She described how her late husband discovered a shop where nine old men were making stirrups. George began working there and then purchased the shop with the income he made. "My father, Clarence Moore (a minister) was good at mechanical things, so he came to work with us," Esther added. Thus, in 1945, the Jetters founded Fort Recovery Industries in Fort Recovery, Ohio.

As funds increased, George looked for ways to serve God financially. George recalled LeTourneau's example, that God had helped him give 90 percent of his income and live on 10 percent. George highly valued education, having been the first in his family to attend college. He was on the founding board of Mount Vernon Nazarene University and helped choose the site. The Jetters subsequently provided funds that helped build the Free Enterprise Business Center and the Jennie K. Moore Family and Consumer Sciences Center. They also established the Jetter Mission Endowed Scholarship to educate future leaders and hired or even housed students.

As the business grew they desired to extend their giving even more. Esther said, "A missionary, Louise Robinson Chapman, suggested, 'Why not give for a church for each of your children?'" They liked the idea and gave money to build a church and parsonage in South Africa in honor of each of their four sons and three daughters, then gave money for an eighth! "In the last two years of his life, George had a passion for water projects," Esther noted.

The couple faithfully prayed for their children, grandchildren, and great-grandchildren, and many pursued degrees or are currently enrolled at Christian universities. The heritage represents a variety of careers, including a pastor, a missionary, lawyers, doctors, artists, and educators. The Jetters' offspring caught their global vision and continue to support ministries and mission initiatives in Africa, Central America, South America, and the Middle East.

Today, stirrup making is a distant memory, but with a workforce of more than three hundred employees, the Fort Recovery–based business is a manufacturer of die cast hardware and components for manufacturers worldwide. Three of the Jetters' sons run the business; the fourth is a minister.

Although the Jetters made enough money to live comfortably, they never spent it on an extravagant lifestyle. "I didn't realize how wise he was until after he died," Esther said, noting George was astute at stocks, bonds, and land deals. He would give the property to schools, churches, and the like, and saved income on behalf of his family.

John Wesley advocated taking care of your family first, then giving your money away. In one year George Jetter made the equivalent of $1.4 million, and lived on 2 percent of his income, giving away 98 percent.

"George believed some people should be called to give and some called to live the life of a missionary," Esther reflected. "I do think the message needs to go out to our young people that if you have the proper attitude about money, it can be a blessing."

Reflection Questions

1. Is your current work situation promoting a sense of personal well-being to you and your co-workers?
2. Consider ways you could bring change to the workplace.
3. In what circumstances would you walk away from an unhealthy job?

For Further Reading

Kelloway, E. Kevin, and Arla L. Day. "Building Healthy Workplaces: What We Know So Far." *Canadian Journal of Behavioural Science/Revue canadienne des sciences du comportement* 37, no. 4 (2005): 223–35. doi: 10.1037/h0087259. Also, http://ohpsychology.ca/wp-content /uploads/2011/02/day-kelloway-1.pdf.

LaBier, Douglas. "The Lowdown on Abusive Bosses and the Unhealthy Workplace—Part 1." *Psychology Today*, June 25, 2011. http:// www.psychologytoday.com/blog/the-new-resilience/201106/the -lowdown-abusive-bosses-and-the-unhealthy-workplace-part-1. For more on the referenced 2011 poll, see the Psychologically Healthy Workplace Program website, http://www.phwa.org/.

NgTrader. "The History of Boots the Chemist—Nottingham." http:// ngtrader.co.uk/thebootsstory.htm. Also see Books UK, Alliance Boots. "Boots History." http://www.boots-uk.com/About_Boots /Boots_Heritage/Boots_History.aspx.

People Bottomline. http://www.thepeoplebottomline.com/. Formerly the Worktrauma.org website.

Randy Maddox. "The Holistic Vision of John Wesley: Q&A with Randy Maddox Part I" Interview by John Shorb. *Church Health Reader*, October 25, 2010. http://chreader.org/contentPage.aspx?resource _id=580.

Sauter, Steven L., Lawrence R. Murphy, and Joseph J. Hurrell. "Prevention of Work-Related Psychological Disorders: A National Strategy Proposed by the National Institute for Occupational Safety and Health (NIOSH)." *American Psychologist* 45, no. 10 (1990): 1146–58. doi: 10.1037/0003-066X.45.10.1146.

Wesley, John. "Heaviness through Manifold Temptations." 1 Peter 1:6 (sermon, n.p., n.d.). In *Sermons of John Wesley, 1872 Edition*. Edited by Thomas Jackson. Wesley Center Online. http://wesley.nnu.edu /john-wesley/the-sermons-of-john-wesley-1872-edition/sermon -47-heaviness-through-manifold-temptations/.

———. "The More Excellent Way." 1 Corinthians 12:31 (sermon, n.p., 1787). In *Sermons of John Wesley, 1872 Edition*. Edited by Thomas Jackson. Wesley Center Online. http://wesley.nnu.edu/john-wesley /the-sermons-of-john-wesley-1872-edition/sermon-89-the-more -excellent-way/.

———. *Primitive Physick: or, An Easy and Natural Method of Curing Most Diseases.* London: G. Woodfall, 1747. http://www.umcmission.org /Find-Resources/Global-Worship-and-Spiritual-Growth/The-Wesleys -and-Their-Times/Primitive-Physick. Wesley first published his book anonymously in 1747 (2nd ed.). Not until 1760 (8th ed.) did he place his name on it.

———. "Upon Our Lord's Sermon on the Mount: Discourse Three." Matthew 5:8–12 (sermon, n.p., n.d.). In *Sermons of John Wesley, 1872 Edition.* Edited by Thomas Jackson. Wesley Center Online. http://wesley .nnu.edu/john-wesley/the-sermons-of-john-wesley-1872-edition /sermon-23-upon-our-lords-sermon-on-the-mount-discourse-three/.

Workplace Bullying Institute. "Who Gets Targeted." June 22, 2011. http:// www.workplacebullying.org/individuals/problem/who-gets -targeted/.

Workplace Bullying Institute, and Gary Namie. *2010 WBI U.S. Workplace Bullying Survey.* Conducted by Zogby International. Bellingham, WA: Workplace Bullying Institute, 2010. http://www.workplacebullying .org/wbiresearch/2010-wbi-national-survey/.

Work That Promotes Social and Economic Well-Being

5

> The Gospel of Christ knows of no religion,
> but social; no holiness but social holiness.
>
> **John Wesley**

One of the most enduring principles of the global Wesleyan movement grew from John Wesley's deep conviction that there is no such thing as solitary religion.

One of his most famous statements is this one:

> "Holy solitaries" is a phrase no more consistent with the Gospel than holy adulterers.

He went further:

> The Gospel of Christ knows of no religion, but social; no holiness but social holiness. Faith working by love is the length and breadth and depth of Christian perfection. This commandment we have from Christ that he who loves God, must love his brother also . . . [We must] manifest our love by doing good unto all . . . especially to them that are of the household of faith. ("Preface," in John Wesley and Charles Wesley, *Hymns and Sacred Poems* [London: W. Strahan, 1739], v–vi)

Through his teaching and his actions John Wesley ensured that this conviction became one of the strongest identifying characteristics of the Wesleyan movement. Christians discipled in this movement were, and are, called to work in ways that promote community well-being.

Our spiritual heritage teaches us that our discipleship of personal spiritual growth actually has its application in the discipleship of community service.

Wesleyans, when they are most faithful to their roots, are committed to understanding what makes communities healthy. They are committed to create and run institutions, businesses, and organizations that make communities healthy places. They engage in the public work that creates and sustains healthy communities. Wesleyans are called to work that promotes community well-being.

The Wesleyan Movement and the Cornish Mining Industry

We don't have space here to do more than give a couple of examples of how this principle worked itself out in the Wesleyan movement of Wesley's day. One of the most intriguing examples is the way that the movement made its impact on the metal mining communities of Cornwall in the south of England.

The Cornish Mining World Heritage Site, while not a religious organization, pays tribute on their website to the way that the Wesleyan movement made Cornish mining communities better places.

> Methodism spoke to the Cornish people in a language they could understand and helped them to make sense of a rapidly changing world. Chapels became the hub of the community in most Cornish mining towns and villages, bringing people together for social events as well as services.

The Wesleyan movement, because it engaged common people in their own language, at their own locations, and addressed the actual pressing issues they were facing, wove itself into the fabric of local communities. This gave hope to people who faced seemingly overwhelming circumstances that seemed far beyond their power to control.

> Methodism was very much a community faith; meetings were held in cottages and barns which made services easily accessible and ideally suited to the close-knit societies that were formed around Cornish metal mining. The domestic setting helped integrate spirituality and rationality with Cornish indigenous folk beliefs. . . .
>
> This important message brought comfort, hope and security to a population that faced daily dangers in the hazardous environment of metal mines and increasing uncertainty in a world being rapidly reshaped by industrialisation.

The Wesleyan movement made these communities better simply by creating networks and links for communication, analysis, accountability, and action. It was a movement centered in the connections between people. People felt included. They were enabled to take ownership of their lives, their families, and their communities.

> These small groups of early Methodists were closely bound together by a word-of-mouth network and the constant movements of itinerants and lay preachers, who were able to travel and interact with different communities in ways that would have been near impossible for the Anglican clergy, who were tied to the church building itself. The use of charismatic lay preachers, like Billy Bray, who preached to the people in the dialect they spoke, gave people [a] sense of social inclusion. Huge crowds were drawn to open-air meetings, and Wesley preached to hundreds at a time in places such as Gwennap Pit.

One of the most interesting factors illustrated by the Cornish mining communities was the connection between the Wesleyan movement and the mining businesses themselves. The movement did not oppose the businesses. Instead, it engaged both the business and the people who worked in them. The Wesleyan message, meetings, and organizations gave confidence to the people working in the businesses, and helped those who led the businesses to do so in ways that made their communities more healthy.

> The link between mining and Methodism was strengthened by the role played by the newly emerging entrepreneurial and merchant class, which was becoming particularly conspicuous where the influence of the Anglican Church was already in decline. Numerous mine captains were also Methodist preachers who communicated to their communities the powerful messages of respectability and self-improvement, thus helping to ensure that Methodism became the most relevant religious institution for labourers and the working class.

This is an example of one of the most enduring features of the Wesleyan view of work. Wesleyans embrace the meaningful work that is present in a community. Wesleyans find ways to create meaningful and rewarding work that helps to ensure that community needs are met.

Wesleyans and the Business of Making Communities Better through Learning

John Wesley's lifelong commitment to learning is another powerful illustration of the Wesleyan movement's commitment to community well-being. Wesley was himself a highly educated person. He enjoyed the best education that eighteenth-century England could provide. He read widely all of his life. His journals show that his own intellectual interests ranged far and wide and never diminished even late in his life.

This is interesting because, unlike so many highly educated people, Wesley didn't confine his interactions to people like himself. He believed, and clearly enjoyed, moving freely and purposefully across all social and intellectual classes.

There is an interesting correspondence between John Wesley and a wealthy, highly educated woman named Miss J. C. March. She was captivated by the Wesleyan message and wanted to experience full salvation. But when Wesley told her that she would be greatly blessed and helped in this if she would visit the poor, she objected. She told him she believed that she should associate with "people of taste and good character." Wesley's response is revealing.

> I have found some of the uneducated poor who have exquisite taste and sentiment; and many, very many, of the rich who have scarcely any at all . . . I want you to converse more . . . with the poorest of the people, who, if they have not taste, have souls, which you may forward in their way to heaven. And they have (many of them) faith and the love of God in a larger measure than any persons I know. Creep in among these in spite of dirt and an hundred disgusting circumstances, and thus put off the gentlewoman. Do not confine your conversation to genteel and elegant people. I should like this as well as you do; but I cannot discover a precedent for it in the life of our Lord or any of His Apostles. (John Wesley to Miss March, 7 February 1776, London)

Clearly John Wesley did not value associating with poor and uneducated people simply because this was a way he could gain the personal benefit of spiritual blessing. He spent time with people of all classes because he genuinely valued and enjoyed them. He saw, despite their difficult circumstances, the great value in people who were often pushed to the margins of society, and blamed for their own difficult circumstances.

The Wesleyan movement embraced the task of working in ways that helped people like this better themselves, and thus, better their communities. For Wesley, learning was a powerful tool in this work.

In an *Isis* journal article titled "John Wesley and Science in 18th Century England," history professor Robert Schofield noted the fact that movements that work with poor and less well-educated people can take on anti-intellectual tendencies. Wesley, though, would have none of this.

> Wesley was disturbed lest his "Methodists" follow that pattern . . . Wesley denied the criticism that Methodism taught the rejection of human learning—adding, characteristically, that learning was "highly expedient for a guide of souls" though not absolutely necessary. He insisted that ". . . the author of our nature designed that we should not destroy but regulate our desire for knowledge"; and "It cannot be that the people will grow in grace unless they give themselves to reading. A reading people will always be a knowing people." (332)

This pursuit of learning for his great movement illustrates a couple of interesting facts about the way John Wesley viewed work that bettered the community. On the one hand, he was passionately committed to calling the members of the movement to learn. On the other hand, he did this by the entrepreneurial creation of a publishing enterprise.

> It is not, therefore, surprising that Wesley took steps in support of his convictions. He encouraged schooling for all of his followers and especially for his lay-preachers. He established schools and reading classes, supervising their curricula and recommending reading lists for those schools and for those

of a similar type started by others. Finally, he started his own printing plant where he printed books that he could recommend. As a writer, editor, publisher, and printer, he was probably not equaled by any other person in England. (Ibid.)

Wesley's publishing enterprise was enormously successful. It made Wesley very wealthy. Some estimate he earned as much as £30,000 (more than $6 million today) over his life from this highly successful entrepreneurial business. He kept none of this money for himself. All but the barest of necessities was reinvested in the work of the movement. We will learn more about this in the next chapter.

The point here is that this work illustrates two foundational characteristics of the Wesleyan movement and its approach to work.

First, Wesleyans engage the people of their communities, particularly those people who live on the margins. By spending time with these people, Wesleyans learn crucial aspects and gain valuable perspectives about the needs of their communities.

Second, Wesleyans embrace all kinds of creative ways to meet those needs, including by starting entrepreneurial businesses and nonprofit organizations.

In this way, Wesleyans live out their calling to do work that promotes community well-being.

Learning Wesleyan Lessons in Haiti

When I (David) was twenty-six, I moved to Haiti to work. It was, and remains, the most challenging personal and professional experience of my life.

Haiti stretched and taxed me in every way. Most of all, Haiti challenged my assumptions and gave me reason to dig deeply into the factors that make communities healthy and unhealthy. Haiti is where I truly learned the power of work, and the crushing effects on communities when they cannot sustain meaningful and rewarding work. Haiti is where I saw in action the organic link between the structures and ideas that lie at the heart of a community, and the ability of that community to sustain meaningful and rewarding work. Haiti was where I began to learn the reality of the Wesleyan principles of work we have been exploring here.

When I went to Haiti I was no stranger to the grimmer realities of life in the poorer communities of our world. I was born in a missionary hospital in one of the poorest neighborhoods of Manila. I grew up in small, poor villages in the rural provinces of the Philippines. I was no stranger to poverty. But Haiti seemed different somehow.

The Haitian people are a marvel of good humor and relentless hope in a world of endless vulnerability. The land is spare and beautiful, though it is ravished by ecological disasters caused by natural and human forces. Haiti has its own culture, a fascinating and vibrant blend of African, Caribbean, European, and American influences.

Not too long after we arrived, my wife and I began to experience something that we hadn't encountered before. Once we were settled in our home a steady stream of visitors came to see us. They were almost always polite and friendly, showing genuine interest in and care for us. Our neighbors welcomed us to their country with genuine warmth. But before every conversation ended our visitors would share a story of hardship and need, and then they would ask if we could help them. This happened so regularly we grew to expect it. This predictable turn of conversation became uncomfortable, but we did our best to respond with help where we could.

Eventually, however, I began to ask questions. Why was this so much a feature of Haitian life? I began to observe as widely and carefully as I could, given my limited knowledge at the time. Clearly most Haitians were painfully poor. But unlike the poor places of my upbringing, Haitians were not just poor in that they lacked material possessions. The deeper I looked, the more I saw my neighbors struggling with a more fundamental poverty. They lived with a desperate vulnerability to natural threats such as hunger, illness, and natural disasters. Yet even deeper, they lived with a vulnerability to political conflict and to exploitation by powerful interests.

Most Haitians lived in unstable and vulnerable houses. Their communities lacked the means to create and sustain stable transportation, communication, energy, health care, and education infrastructures. I watched them cope heroically with these vulnerabilities. And they asked for my help. In the course of time I soon realized that while many asked for specific things such as money, medicine, clothing, and food, there was one thing they asked for far more than any other. They asked for work.

My Haitian neighbors either asked if there was work they could do for me or they asked if I could provide them with resources to start their own entrepreneurial work. I came to realize that my Haitian friends really did not want charity—not from me, not from foreign governments, not from their own government. They wanted to work. There was something natural and organic and untutored in this request. They didn't ask for work because their political ideology told them they should. They asked for work because they wanted to work.

I went to Haiti with the assumption that God somehow, in ways I had never quite discovered, rewards faithful Christians with a good standard of living. Haiti with its many Christian poor plainly showed me that this was not always true. I went to Haiti with the assumption that churches, communities, and countries grow strong through spiritual revivals. Haiti plainly showed me that this is true, but not quite in the way I had assumed. Though I would have denied these assumptions at the time, Haiti forced me to discover certain powerful truths inherent in my Wesleyan tradition that perhaps I already "knew" yet somehow they remained unrealized in my understanding.

I had been well prepared to teach spiritual subjects like Bible, theology, and church leadership. I had no preparation at all to understand the ways that communities work, the factors that shape healthy communities, the needs that we are called to address, and the devastating consequences of communities' inability to sustain the structures that make meaningful, rewarding work possible.

I could help Haitian Christians with spiritual factors. Yet I had no working understanding of the power of my own heritage—John Wesley's insistence that we should sit with the poor and thereby seek to understand their situation; that we should work to create structures and mechanisms that give them understanding, voice, and empowerment in shaping their communities; that we should encourage them in the creation of businesses and organizations that naturally create wealth and thus build the infrastructures that sustain healthy societies.

A powerful insight I learned by sitting with my neighbors in Haiti is that John Wesley was right about people. Haitians are bright, creative, industrious people. In my experience, although their understanding can always be improved with careful learning, poor people are aware of the broken mechanisms that keep their communities unhealthy. Left to their own devices, they will most of the time choose industry, entrepreneurialism, and personal ownership over charity and dependency.

Perhaps the most powerful insight I learned in Haiti is the absolute importance of the social systems and structures in which people live. The power of the economic and legal system either to destroy or to enable meaningful work, to decimate a community or to empower a community to thrive, simply cannot be overstated. It is a high priority for societies to protect the efficacy of the weak and the vulnerable: When their efficacy is taken away from them they are robbed of dignity and they are institutionally prohibited from serving their fellow man and from providing for their own needs. In order for people and communities to thrive a wide variety of business and civil institutions need to be created to solve the underlying economic and social problems.

It is beyond the scope of this book to explore the nature of healthy political, legal, and economic frameworks. But Daron Acemoglu and James Robinson have provided one of the most insightful and instructive studies on the question of why some nations thrive and others struggle with pervasive poverty that seems impervious to change. These two researchers, the former an economist from MIT and the latter a political scientist and economist from Harvard, set out to discover and explain the mechanisms behind this phenomenon.

Their book, *Why Nations Fail*, outlines their basic findings.

> We live in an unequal world . . . In rich countries, individuals are healthier, live longer, and are much better educated. They also have access to a range of amenities and options in life, from vacations to career paths, that people in poor countries can only dream of. People in rich countries also drive on roads without potholes, and enjoy toilets, electricity and running water in their houses. They also typically have governments that do not arbitrarily arrest or harass them; on the contrary, the governments provide services, including education, health care, roads, and law and order. Notable, too, is the fact that the citizens vote in elections and have some voice in the political direction their countries take. (40–41)

What, they ask, explains these differences? They point out popular current theories. One theory is the "geography hypothesis," which says that "the great divide between rich and poor countries is created by geographical differences" (48). Many of the world's poor countries are in tropical climates, while many of the world's richer countries are in temperate climates. This hypothesis doesn't hold up to careful study.

Another is the "culture hypothesis," which says that national prosperity can be traced to sets of beliefs, values, and ethics, much of which rests on religious foundations (57). Culture, they note, is important and can have an impact on the way nations develop. But culture is not an adequate explanation for why some nations develop and maintain prosperity and others remain locked in poverty.

A third popular hypothesis is the "ignorance hypothesis," which says that some countries remain poor because they and their leaders simply do not know how to manage their countries so as to produce wealth (63–64). Further, the world's wealthy countries do not know how to share their knowledge appropriately. But this hypothesis does not hold up, and doesn't adequately explain why nations fail.

Acemoglu and Robinson propose an entirely different explanation that is both enlightening and encouraging.

> Countries differ in their economic success because of their different institutions, the rules influencing how the economy works, and the incentives that motivate people. . . . Inclusive economic institutions . . . are those that allow and encourage participation by the great mass of people in economic activities that make best use of their talents and skills and that enable individuals to make the choices they wish. To be inclusive, economic institutions must feature secure private property, an unbiased system of law, and a provision of public services that provides a level playing field in which people can exchange and contract; it also must permit

the entry of new businesses and allow people to choose their careers. (73–75)

Communities that provide these kinds of institutions build the foundation for well-being, because in these communities people can use their God-given creativity, talents, and hard work to create and spread value widely among themselves and their neighbors. On the other hand, communities in which such institutions are prevented from developing, or are inhibited, extract value and diminish well-being.

I saw these lessons at work firsthand in Haiti. Haiti taught me the inherent value of work and the God-given hunger that all people have to do meaningful and rewarding work. But it also taught me that this individual need to express the image of God in us through meaningful work must be placed within a fair and beneficial political, legal, and economic framework. Without a fair and dependable court system that ensured that the basic virtues of honesty, fairness, and ownership would be followed by everyone, individual Haitians struggled to turn their creativity and their hard work into value for themselves, their families, and their fellow Haitians. Without a banking system that ensured that money could be protected and that money could be borrowed on fair and workable terms to build small businesses, Haitians did not have the working capital to turn their ideas into viable businesses that could provide for their own needs and provide the goods and services their neighbors needed.

Haiti is where I began to learn the power of my own heritage and its view of work. It is where I began to see the power of systems that I had always taken for granted even though I grew up as a missionary kid living under impoverished conditions.

At the heart of our Wesleyan heritage is a commitment to the well-being of communities and an understanding that it is in the pursuit of this well-being that God teaches us the most important lessons about our own spiritual maturity.

Characteristics of Healthy Communities

Before we leave this exploration of the Wesleyan commitment to community well-being, we should briefly summarize some key characteristics of healthy and unhealthy communities.

Harvard sociology professor William Julies Wilson has done extensive research in urban communities where work has disappeared. He found that all communities that cannot sustain meaningful, stable work eventually take on certain social and personal features with undesirable consequences. In communities where work disappears:

Social organization declines. Structures and activities that link members of a community together begin to disappear. Community members become isolated, retreating into cocoons of silence and disengagement. The public commons falls into disrepair.

Social integration disappears. Communities without work have less socioeconomic diversity. Healthy communities are made up of people and families of various economic, educational, and professional statuses. Role models are available for children to observe. Patterns of productive behavior are reinforced even for those who may be going through hard times. Businesses and service organizations locate in the community. But when work disappears all of these characteristics begin to disappear, changing forever the look and essence of the community.

Community makeup changes. Businesses and service agencies move out. Schools struggle to find resources and to attract and retain top-quality teachers. The physical infrastructure falls into disrepair.

Illegitimate behavior increases. Dysfunctional, illegal, and antisocial behaviors tend to increase when work disappears from a community. In time, left unchecked, these behaviors come to define a community, feeding a spiral of violence, fear, and decay.

Personal apathy increases. As the situation worsens, those who remain in the community adopt a crippling sense of apathy. The problems seem so deep-rooted and the solutions so unattainable that even those who wish for something better, give up.

Wilson published his research and findings listed above in *When Work Disappears: The World of the New Urban Poor.* In this work he also said,

> The consequences of high neighborhood joblessness are more devastating than those of high neighborhood poverty. A neighborhood in which people are poor but employed is different from a neighborhood in which people are poor and jobless. Many of today's problems in the inner-city ghetto neighborhoods—crime, family dissolution, welfare, low levels of social organization, and so on—are fundamentally a consequence of the disappearance of work. (xiii)

These are the factors we can observe the Wesleyan movement addressing in eighteenth-century England. They are the factors that our Wesleyan commitment to community well-being should lead us to address today no matter where they exist in the world.

Our theological heritage helps us to see that there is a connection between the ideas that lie at the heart of communities and the health of those communities. Part of our discipleship challenge is to work in ways that encourage people to embrace ideas that promote healthy communities.

What are the conditions that best allow communities to create and sustain meaningful and rewarding work? Here are four ideas that we can observe in our movement and that scholarship and experience link to healthy communities.

Virtue

Virtue is absolutely essential. In particular, there must be a certain level of trust involved in every business and organizational transaction that takes place. Whether we go to the store and hand cash to the cashier to buy groceries, or whether we put our credit card number online, there is always an element of trust. Trust is absolutely essential to the healthy functioning of communities. It is remarkable how much one can see elements in the Wesleyan movement that build networks of trust to counteract the challenges that came with the industrialization of England in the eighteenth century. Much of this trust is so implicit that we don't even think about it. But it is absolutely essential to the healthy functioning of communities. Trust is everywhere. A primary mechanism that communities need in order to protect the principles that build trust is the protections and provisions of law and order, proper authority, and justice.

Rule of Law

Thus the second system that is essential in healthy communities is the rule of law. The rule of law simply means that the law will be enforced equally and fairly among all the participants regardless of any other characteristics that may apply to them. If trust is violated somehow either by inattention or by deceit, in a healthy community neighbors can then appeal to the rule of law. If the businesses we create decide not to pay our workers, they may appeal to the law. If the customers our businesses serve refuse to pay, we may appeal to the law. In healthy communities laws are seen to be fair and applicable to all equally. When laws are passed that privilege one group over another, problems inevitably arise.

Ownership Rights

Ownership rights are another essential element necessary for healthy communities. John Wesley taught the members of the Methodist movement that, ultimately, all property belongs to God. We are simply stewards of the things God has given us. Nevertheless, the movement operated on the assumption that healthy communities enshrine the principle that individuals hold and use private property responsibly, indeed, in ways in keeping with God's purpose. The Wesleyan movement worked to shape healthy communities where members worked to create wealth, use it wisely, and invest it in the greater good of the community.

Ethic of Value Creation

Societies that manage to nurture a shared ethic that honors the creation of value lay the groundwork for widespread well-being. This ethic rests ultimately on the biblical command that we are to love our neighbors as ourselves. Value creation occurs when people use their creativity, knowledge, insight, and work to create things that are of value, that others need and want. This process reflects the genius of God's creation. It benefits those who do it and it spreads benefit throughout a community. Societies that honor this principle, that provide systemic and institutional frameworks which encourage it, and that reward it appropriately lay the groundwork for community well-being.

So now, with that overview, is it possible for anyone to embody this kind of commitment to community well-being? Yes it is. Meet Keith Stanton of Christchurch, New Zealand.

> I want the whole Christ for my Savior, the whole Bible for my book, the whole Church for my fellowship, and the whole world for my mission field.
>
> John Wesley

The Thirst Quencher

It began with planning a summer holiday in 1988. Keith Stanton of Christchurch, New Zealand, told his wife, "'I would like to go and travel to some exotic place,' and she said, 'Well, I'm not going anywhere there's not clean toilets!'" They discussed going on tour with World Vision, where their time would be spent visiting projects and sightseeing. "We decided World Vision wouldn't give us any rubbishy accommodations!" he laughed.

On that first tour the Stantons visited a village in Bangladesh where World Vision had installed a school, water supply, and sanitation system. Previously, the village of about six thousand had been losing a majority of children before the age of five due to waterborne diseases. The women were concerned about their future, so Keith donated fifty pedal sewing machines with which they could start a business. He relayed, "Eighteen months later, we received in the mail a big parcel of clothing!" A couple of years later, six hundred people were involved in the village's worldwide export clothing business.

"From then on it was water; I was motivated really by that first story, how water changed the lives of these people in this village, and also provided the opportunity for children to grow and develop into mature adulthood." At last count, Keith has supported 346 water projects in sixteen countries, mostly in Africa.

Keith's grandfather was a Methodist home missionary who went on to be a director for the China Inland Mission. But with thirteen children to support, his grandfather eventually started a stationery and printing business. Keith worked there with his father, and at the age of forty-five, established his own business. "That's really where I got the funds from to start the projects," he explained.

"Wesley was a great encourager of people to go and to make money and to use it to help others. And that was part of the philosophy that came down through my upbringing." But there was a time when the Methodist Church in New Zealand frowned upon people who were in business. "They felt people's money was an evil thing. I don't know where that idea came from; it's not true, because without money you can't do too much to help others. I always had the feeling it was there to share, there to help."

By 2002 Keith had sold the business and decided to visit some of the projects. "I wanted to make sure the money was being well spent and was fulfilling the needs, that it would go on and serve the people for years." At the age of seventy-eight, Keith is still at it. His latest water project will provide about fourteen thousand people with clean water. He is also building a school in Tanzania and has funded Wesleyan Methodist church buildings.

"[Giving] is good for the receiver and it's also good for the giver," he stated. "The satisfaction I get out of it is actually seeing the smiling faces of the children, and seeing people have the opportunity to grow and live a life of fulfillment."

Perhaps most importantly, Keith's lifelong commitment to creating viable businesses that were focused on meeting the needs of the people his business could serve was rewarded with the creation of wealth. Keith's lifelong commitment to the Wesleyan principles of discipline, self-control, and thriftiness allowed him to have resources he could give away. God used his faithfulness to bless others through two powerful means—his wonderful charitable spirit and his ability to create sustainable businesses that produce well-being for others and wealth that he could put toward good uses.

Keith's story aptly illustrates the discipleship principles embedded in the Wesleyan heritage.

Reflection Questions

1. How does what you do benefit others?
2. How does what others do benefit you?

3. What needs do you see in your community?

4. What skills do you have or could you develop that could meet those needs?

For Further Reading

Acemoglu, Daron, and James A. Robinson. *Why Nations Fail: The Origins of Power, Prosperity and Poverty.* New York: Crown Business, Random House, 2012.

Cornish Mining World Heritage Site. "Religion." http://www.cornish-mining .org.uk/delving-deeper/religion.

Maddox, Randy L. "'Visit the Poor': John Wesley, the Poor, and the Sanctification of Believers." In Richard P. Heitzenrater, ed. *The Poor and the People Called Methodists, 1729–1999.* Nashville: Kingswood Books, 2002.

Schofield, Robert E. "John Wesley and Science in 18th Century England." *Isis* 44, no. 4 (1953): 331–40.

Wilson, William J. *When Work Disappears: The World of the New Urban Poor.* New York: Knopf, 1996.

Wesley, John. John Wesley to Miss March, 7 February 1776, London. In *The Letters of John Wesley.* Vol. 6. Edited by John Telford. London: Epworth Press, 1931. Wesley Center Online. http://wesley.nnu.edu /john-wesley/the-letters-of-john-wesley/wesleys-letters-1776/. Also quoted in Maddox, "'Visit the Poor'" cited above.

———. "Preface." In John Wesley and Charles Wesley. *Hymns and Sacred Poems.* London: W. Strahan, 1739. Vol. 14 of *The Works of John Wesley.* Edited by Thomas Jackson. London: Wesleyan-Methodist Book Room, 1872.

Work That Is an Expression of Christian Compassion

6

A Methodist [Christian] is one who loves the
Lord his God with all his heart, with all his soul,
with all his mind, and with all his strength.

John Wesley

Having, First, gained all you can, and, Secondly
saved all you can, Then "give all you can."

John Wesley

Proceed with much prayer, and your way
will be made plain.

John Wesley

J ohn Wesley's home in London is an unremark-
able row house perched unobtrusively next to the more
familiar and more photogenic Wesley's Chapel. Though these
buildings are not famous tourist stops they are fascinating and
meaningful destinations for those whose lives have been shaped
by the Wesleyan heritage. On the second floor of the home is Wesley's bedroom and adjacent to that is his prayer room.

When I lived and worked in England I visited several times.
When you visit the Chapel and the home, the sense of Wesley's

spare, tidy, functional life comes through. My favorite place to visit was the little prayer room next to Wesley's bedroom. It is just a few paces from his bed. His own records show that he was scrupulous in his habits of prayer and Bible reading. I can only imagine the hours he spent in this room praying for the worldwide movement that bore his name and embodied his convictions.

Whenever I stood in this little prayer room my mind would wander out over the breadth and depth of the worldwide family of John Wesley churches. I once felt overcome with emotion when I realized that in a sense, though he could never have imagined me and my family, still I was touched by the prayers prayed in that little room.

There I stood, before a simple kneeling bench in the tidy little room in London, a world and an eon of time away from the little Philippine barrio where I grew up. Yet my own life's journey had been shaped by the prayers made in that little alcove. Never before nor since have I felt so powerfully the global legacy of the Wesleyan movement. Nor have I seen so clearly as then that the Wesleyan movement was born, came to maturity, and continues today through the power of prayer.

But what came most powerfully to my mind and heart in that little prayer room, was the realization that the motivating force behind that prayer life, was a heart full of love for millions of people that John Wesley would never know. This was not a human love. John Wesley was an extraordinary man, a great man by the standards of this world. But he was a man. The love that flowed through his ministry, that called to life a movement that literally changed the world, was a gift from God.

Wesley was often asked to describe the unique characteristics of the people of the Wesleyan movement. In 1742 he wrote a tract called *The Character of a Methodist* in which he attempted to describe the members of the movement.

He wrote about what does *not* describe the movement.

1. The distinguishing marks of a Methodist are not his opinions of any sort. His assenting to this or that scheme of religion, his embracing any particular set of notions, his espousing the judgment of one man or of another, are all quite wide of the point. *[What defines our movement is not our opinions about controversial issues.]*

2. Neither are words or phrases of any sort. We do not place our religion, or any part of it, in being attached to any peculiar mode of speaking, any quaint or uncommon set of expressions. *[What defines our movement is not some special theological formulation of ideas or expression of religious ideas.]*

3. Nor do we desire to be distinguished by actions, customs, or usages, of an indifferent nature. Our religion does not lie in doing what God has not enjoined, or abstaining from what he hath not forbidden. It does not lie in the form of our apparel, in the posture of our body, or the covering of our heads; nor yet in abstaining from marriage, or from meats and drinks, which are all good if received with thanksgiving. *[What defines our movement is not what we do or don't do, how we dress or don't dress, what we eat or don't eat.]*

4. Nor, lastly, is he distinguished by laying the whole stress of religion on any single part of it. *[What defines our movement is not some special emphasis on one distinctive teaching.]*

So what is it then? What is the central defining characteristic of our movement? Here is the best summary of his answer.

What then is the mark?

A Methodist is one who has "the love of God shed abroad in his heart by the Holy Ghost given to him"; one who "loves the Lord his God with all his heart, and with all his soul, and with all his mind, and with all his strength."

> And while he thus always exercises his love to God . . .
> this commandment is written in his heart, that "he who
> loveth God, loves his brother also."
>
> Lastly, as he has time, he "does good unto all men"—
> unto neighbors and strangers, friends, and enemies. And
> that in every possible kind; not only to their bodies, by "feed-
> ing the hungry, clothing the naked, visiting those that are
> sick or in prison," but much more does he labor to do good to
> their souls, as of the ability which God giveth. (Wesley, *Char-
> acter of a Methodist*)

Think about this for a moment. The Wesleyan movement was
never meant to be distinguished by the elegance of its theological
formulations, by the purity of its behavioral codes, by the powerful promotion of carefully reasoned opinions about secondary issues of the day. Instead the movement was always intended to be
distinguished by the reality of conversion that bore fruit in holiness of heart and life. And that holiness was always intended to be
expressed in unstinting, practical works of mercy and grace, given
freely, creatively, and abundantly to the world's most needy people.

This was the genius of the movement. It is the genius that
shapes a Wesleyan understanding of the discipleship of work.
Wesleyans are called to do work that is the expression of Christian
compassion. This certainly can mean work that we have come to
associate with nonprofit charities. But it means much more.

This speaks to the motivation that is to lie at the heart of all
kinds of organizations and all kinds of work. It does not speak of
the form of the organizations. This means that in the Wesleyan
view, godly work is not defined by what one does but by the way
one does it. This means that the work of entrepreneurs, artists,
architects, builders, financiers, doctors, lawyers, teachers, farm-
ers, groundskeepers, housekeepers, cooks, administrators, managers, and cubicle-dwellers of all kinds—all of these forms of
work may be sanctified, made whole, and holy, and prosperous, by

the motivation from which they are undertaken.

Perhaps nothing makes this point more powerfully than John Wesley's most famous and most practical message on the use of money. We must put this message in its proper context in order to understand it. In their anthology titled *John Wesley's Sermons*, theology professor Albert Outler and church history and Wesley studies professor Richard Heitzenrater wrote,

> The new capitalism of Wesley's world had resulted in a steady accumulation of venture capital and, correspondingly, a shocking contrast between the splendid lifestyle of the newly rich and the grinding misery of the perennial poor. The impoverished masses were Wesley's self-chosen constituency: "Christ's poor." At the same time, Wesley was deeply committed to a work ethic that saw sloth as sin and that condemned self-indulgence as a faithless stewardship of God's bounties in creation. He did not see money as anything evil in itself. Thrift, industry, honesty, sobriety, generosity were all Christian virtues; their warrants rested in the twin love of God and neighbor, and thus they were included in the agenda of holy living. (347)

Here, in short summary, is Wesley's teaching on the subject after which his sermon is titled, "The Use of Money."

> Perhaps all the instructions which are necessary . . . may be reduced to three plain rules, by the exact observance whereof we may approve ourselves faithful stewards.
>
> The first of these is: *"Gain all you can."* But this it is certain we ought not to do: we ought not to gain money at the expense of life; nor . . . at the expense of our health. We are, secondly, to gain all we can without hurting our mind any more than our body . . . We must preserve, at all events, the spirit of an healthful mind. Therefore we may not engage or continue in any sinful trade, any that is contrary to the law of God, or of our country. We are thirdly to gain all we can

without hurting our neighbor. We cannot, if we love everyone as ourselves, hurt anyone in his substance. Neither may
we gain by hurting our neighbor in his body. [Nor may we
gain] by hurting our neighbor in his soul. Never leave anything till tomorrow that you can do today. And do it as well as
possible. Gain all you can, by common sense, by using in your
business all the understanding which God has given you.

Having gained all you can, by honest wisdom and un-
wearied diligence, the second rule of Christian prudence is:
"Save all you can." Do not waste any part . . . merely in gratifying the desires of the flesh; in procuring the pleasures of
sense of whatever kind. Do not waste any part . . . merely in
gratifying the desire of the eye by superfluous or expensive
apparel, or by needless ornaments. Lay out nothing to grat-
ify the pride of life, to gain the admiration or praise of men.

Having first gained all you can, and secondly saved all
you can, then: *"Give all you can."* First, provide things needful
for yourself—food to eat, raiment to put on, whatever nature
moderately requires for preserving the body in health and
strength. Second, provide these for your wife, your children,
your servants, or any others who pertain to your household.
If when this is done there be an overplus left, then "do good
to them that are of the household of faith." If there be an
overplus still, "as you have opportunity, do good unto all
men." In so doing, you give all you can. ("The Use of Money,"
3; I.1–4, 6–8; II.1–4; III.1, 3, emphasis added)

In these directions we see once again the principles that shape the
Wesleyan understanding of work and economics. The ethic of love
calls us to embrace all of the productive means available to us to
bless our communities and the people who live in them. We are
called specifically to work diligently, creatively, even urgently in
order to gain as much as we can. We are called to do this in ways
that promote personal and community well-being.

Unlike the emerging wealth of the Industrial Revolution that amassed unbelievable fortunes in the hands of a few, the ethic of the Wesleyan movement gave productive work a higher purpose. Wesleyans did not work just to make money, to amass personal fortunes, to satisfy their our own desires, to impress others, or to wield power. They work to make the world a better place to the greater glory of God and the benefit of humanity.

This ethic calls each of us to examine the gifts and the passions of our lives. What contribution can we make with our unique gifts and talents? The Wesleyan movement holds the conviction that wealth can be created. When we gain wealth we are not necessarily depriving others of wealth. Our gains do not necessarily come at the expense of others. In fact, one most often gains wealth by serving the needs of others.

Most of all our productivity and our thrift are put at the service of reinvestment in the well-being of our communities. This is what it means when we say that Wesleyans are called to do work that is motivated by Christian compassion. This is rare. Even in Wesley's day, few gave as he did. So is this a standard that anyone can meet? Meet modern day Wesleyans Tom and Joan Phillippe and Ken Sloane.

> I will be no longer mine own, but give up myself to thy will in all things. . . . I freely and heartily resign all to thy pleasure and disposal.
>
> John Wesley

The Investors

An enriching life of love, ministry, and giving began for Tom and Joan Phillippe when they met in college. He was learning everything he could at Marion College (now Indiana Wesleyan University) to fulfill his calling to be a minster. "My heart's desire was to preach the Word," he stated. "I was careful to choose the right friends and the right girl that I would marry, so that we could work together for the same desires to do God's will in whatever way He would lead us."

Tom became the pastor of Wesleyan churches in Ohio, Minnesota, and Florida. Dr. Joan Phillippe was an educator, while Dr. Tom Phillippe was an evangelist in the Wesleyan Church, associate evangelist for the Billy Graham Evangelistic Association, and served as general director of the Wesleyan Church's Department of Extension and Evangelism. In that role, Tom said, "I oversaw the development and planting of new churches, one of which is now a fifteen thousand member church in Atlanta, Georgia, called 12Stone Church."

While a pastor, it was Tom's habit to share meals with businessmen in his church to help them in any way he could. Fred O'Dell became a business mentor to Tom while he was the pastor of Waite Park Wesleyan Church in Minneapolis. Tom explained: "When there was a need to put some in my congregation in a nursing home, I asked him if he knew of a good place." O'Dell suggested they visit one of his homes. The cleanliness of the home and its residents and the many activities offered intrigued the Phillippes. They were impressed with how the residents were engaged in ministry, for example, making things missionaries needed.

The Phillippes began thinking about investing in nursing homes to help put their children through college. They joined O'Dell in investing in other nursing homes in Minnesota, Indiana, and Ohio and formed Nationwide Management, Inc., to manage and build new nursing homes, assisted living units, apartments, day cares, and other entities. The vision grew beyond educating their kids. Tom said, "My intent was to make as much money as possible so I had much to give to others, not only through our ministry but through our health care facilities. We have been able to give to all of our Wesleyan educational institutions and many churches."

Their whole motive was ministry. Each of their nursing homes had a spiritual atmosphere with a chaplain. "My passion and love for people and God's kingdom has shaped the way I thought about it. God has continued to pour out blessing after blessing because of our faithfulness in giving of our money, ourselves, and our resources."

The Phillippes' generous example has had a ripple effect. Many of the younger men in leadership in their business branched out into businesses of their own and are committing to ministry through giving of their resources. Tom quoted Proverbs 3:5–10 as his favorite Scripture passage. "Trust in the LORD . . . Honor the LORD with your wealth." This results in health, nourishment, and lives overflowing with blessings.

The Steward

Ken Sloane is accustomed to living on half of his income and giving away the rest. "Mike Slaughter at Ginghamsburg UMC is the one who inspired me to 'live simply so that others may simply live,'" began Ken, who lives and works in Nashville, Tennessee.

Eight years ago, a pastor in a church near Dayton, Ohio, challenged people to observe the kind of Christmas that would show "it's not our birthday, it's Jesus' birthday." The story of the transformations that have happened has impacted thousands. Ken explained: "His call to action was to give an amount equal to the amount people spend on Christmas to support the life-saving mission work the church was doing in Sudan. The church has invested more than $5 million in sustainable humanitarian projects since beginning its Christmas Miracle Offering initiative in 2004."

"I was also inspired by the little book *Enough* by Adam Hamilton to set limits on what I want and to find contentment in having the simple things I need," Ken continued. The book, written by a

Methodist pastor, addresses the challenge of how to live as a faithful disciple of Jesus Christ in a consumer-driven world.

"A few years back I went through a divorce, and during that time, trying not to interrupt the lifestyle of my ex-wife and children, I lived for about eighteen months on one thousand dollars per month (about one-seventh of my salary). I shopped carefully at the grocery store, looking for sales and items marked down for quick sale. I went from a 3,600-square-foot house to a 600-square-foot apartment." He started shopping at stores that sold previously owned items. "I was not miserable; in fact, I was happier. When I was with my children (all young adults) we had more good time together than we had experienced in a while."

John Wesley lived on a fraction of his income, advocating living a frugal lifestyle to be able to have more resources to help those in need.

Ken remarried eight months ago. "Prior to this I had purchased a 1,400-square-foot townhouse. Bridget and I are living on less than half of our income. We are tithing and supporting additional projects—pensions for pastors in Africa, food programs here in Nashville, etc.—but we have a financial goal we want to reach, which we believe will empower us both to be able to give even more generously to causes that have captured our hearts. We enjoy shopping for clothes at Goodwill and furnishing our home with furniture from the Habitat Store or Goodwill. I've developed a love for building things, often around items I find at the Habitat Store here in Nashville.

"The bottom line, I guess, is that I've found a joy, contentment, and peace that I haven't known in most of my adult life. And I feel so blessed and am thrilled at the prospect of being a blessing to others."

Rev. Dr. Ken Sloane is director of stewardship for the General Board of Discipleship, The United Methodist Church. He has spent much of his time on the road talking with congregations about connectional giving—churches working together to do what no one church could do alone.

Reflection Questions

1. What gifts and talents has God given you?
2. In what ways can you show the compassion of Christ to others?
3. How will you creatively work to make the world a better place?

For Further Reading

Dayton, Donald W. *Discovering an Evangelical Heritage.* Peabody, MA: Hendrickson, 1988.

Hamilton, Adam. *Enough: Discovering Joy through Simplicity and Generosity.* Nashville: Abingdon, 2009.

Jennings, Theodore W., Jr. *Good News to the Poor: John Wesley's Evangelical Economics.* Nashville: Abingdon, 1990.

Outler, Albert C., and Richard P. Heitzenrater, eds. *John Wesley's Sermons: An Anthology.* Nashville: Abingdon, 1991. Selected sermons originally published in *The Works of John Wesley*, vols. 1–4: Sermons I–IV. Nashville: Abingdon, 1984–87.

Wesley, John. *The Character of a Methodist* (tract, n.p., 1742). In *The Works of John Wesley.* Edited by Thomas Jackson. 14 vols. London, Wesleyan Conference Office, 1872. New York, NY: General Board of Global Ministries, 2012. http://www.umcmission.org/Find-Resources/Global-Worship-and-Spiritual-Growth/The-Wesleys-and-Their-Times/The-Character-of-a-Methodist.

———. "On Charity." 1 Corinthians 13:1–3 (sermon, n.p., n.d.). In *Sermons of John Wesley, 1872 Edition.* Edited by Thomas Jackson. Wesley Center Online. http://wesley.nnu.edu/john-wesley/the-sermons-of-john-wesley-1872-edition/sermon-91-on-charity/.

———. "The Use of Money." Luke 16:9 (sermon, n.p., n.d.). In *Sermons of John Wesley, 1872 Edition*. Edited by Thomas Jackson. Wesley Center Online. http://wesley.nnu.edu/john-wesley/the-sermons-of-john -wesley-1872-edition/sermon-50-the-use-of-money/.

Conclusion

God is so great, that He
communicates greatness to *the least
thing that is done for His service.*

John Wesley (emphasis added)

Oひ ne of my favorite authors was an anthropologist named Colin Turnbull. He taught me so much about people. I wish I could have taken classes from him, but I did the next best thing. I read his enthralling ethnographies of the African and Hindu peoples with whom he had lived.

In his book *The Human Cycle*, Turnbull writes about the lessons he learned from the Mbuti people of Zaire and the Hindus of Benares about the art of living well. The Mbuti are a small people living in central Africa. Their lives were lived almost completely within the confines of the Ituri forest. Turnbull recounts a delightful lesson about work by reflecting on the ways of the Mbuti culture.

"For most of us," Turnbull wrote, "if we are run-of-the-mill adults, adulthood is associated with work more than with play, and for many of us work is little more than drudgery, an obligation we fulfill in order to get enough money to keep us alive. For only a lucky few is work such an integral part of life that the distinction between work and play vanishes, both becoming no more than different ways of manifesting our full potential for the art of living" (*The Human Cycle*, 173).

We may dream of a life in which we do not have to work at all. And there is a way into this dream, but it is not by doing away with work. It is by learning to see work in a completely different way. Instead of being captives to a drudgery whose only purpose is an instrumental one, to make us enough money to keep body and soul together, we must try to live in the place where work becomes the natural and normal expression of the persons God has made us to be.

The curse of the fall was not that we should be doomed to work. The sorrow and curse of the fall was that we should be doomed to experience work as drudgery, frustrating, and painful. The joy and blessing of conversion is not that we are freed from working but that we are freed to experience work as the expression of all that is most beautiful and magnificent about us.

Turnbull wrote further about the possibility of blurring the lines of distinction between work and play such that one or the other is just another way of enacting the art of living, and he said, "In other cultures there is such a way. It is really quite simple. In such cultures 'work' is seen merely as doing whatever you are doing at that particular moment in your life. . . . The art that some of us find in doing whatever we do with equal enjoyment and fun and satisfaction is the art of making sacred and social that which is otherwise secular and individual" (Ibid., 173–74).

Perhaps this is another way of saying just what we have been exploring in this little book on work from a Wesleyan perspective. All too often we allow our culture to frame work as drudgery, a necessary nuisance, and worst of all, a result of God's curse. But as we have seen, in God's plan work is just the opposite. Our ability to work is one of God's greatest gifts to humankind. God has invited us into the majesty of creation, to shape our world, to make our world a better place through our work.

So let me be explicit about my hope for you. I hope you will come to see the beauty, the joy, and the value in the work that God has called you to do. Whether you pass through seasons of drudgery when your work is uninspiring or whether you find yourself in a job you absolutely love—celebrate the person God has called you to be and the worker God has called you to be.

I'd like to leave with a challenge.

Give yourself wholeheartedly to the task of discovering how you are uniquely gifted to make the world a better place through your work. Finding your work is a sacred task. Whether you are young, middle aged, or older, it is never too late to discover how the work you choose to do, in each stage of life, will be used to enrich your own life and to make the world a better place.

Know this. You will be surrounded by a cacophony of voices calling you to many conflicting views about your work. Some will be voices of fear and despair. They will tell you that you are not able to do anything of consequence, that the world will not let you succeed, that the power brokers of this world have stacked the playing field against you, that you are just a pawn being used in the great materialistic power plays of this world's great schemers. They will tell you, sometimes subtly and sometimes overtly, that you are less than human. You are simply "labor" to be used in the self-serving plans of others.

Perhaps the most seductive voices will call you to a lifetime of self-centered pursuit. You may be tempted to choose a job when God wants to give you work that will become a mission. That work may take place on a grand stage or it may play out in a factory or a store where *your* work will make *that* world a better, more humane, more creative, more successful, more enjoyable, more *valuable* place. You may be tempted to build a career when God will give you the circumstances to make a lifetime of difference restoring the people and the communities around you into places that reflect the beauty, bounty, and well-being of God.

No matter what your own personal abilities may be, you have been created in God's image, endowed with gifts, talents, creativity of your own, and a will to seek the best in every situation, to thrive in the midst of chaos and defeat, to take life as it comes to you and make it better. Will you drift with the tides of the times, never dreaming of how you and those who believe in a better future, can turn the tide? Or will you surf the waves and catch the winds to a better world? Will you surrender to apathy? Or will you make your way toward the summit of a chosen purpose? Will you allow your imagination and your aspirations to be frozen in the tomb of cynicism? Or will you allow the small green shoots of purpose and imagination to blossom into a lifetime of achievement?

I have a challenge for those who teach, who preach, who lead organizations. The people who look to you for knowledge, insight, wisdom, courage, and guidance need your help. They need encouragement when circumstances are tough. They need someone to walk alongside in those days when they can't find their work. They need to be reminded of the purpose in their work.

You must use your influence to nurture the kind of economic and legal systems that favor meaningful, rewarding work. You must exercise the leadership that legitimizes, maintains, and creates communities that value work and that value the systems that make work possible and rewarding for the most people—that will discover and nurture the greatest creations of art, inventions of technology or medicine, or organizations of service.

Just as John Wesley lived boldly into a time of great challenge and change, calling wealthy and poor alike to lives of discipline, integrity, ingenuity, and service—so must we do that in our time. We must give people the dignity of work that is meaningful and rewarding. We must use all the influence we have to ensure that the world creates economic, legal, and organizational structures that enable work that truly will make the world a better place.

To my fellow workers, created in God's image and called to make the world a better place through our work—my prayer is that your college or university, your church, your nonprofit organization, your city, your state legislature, your federal government representatives will help you find this purpose for your life's work, that they will give you the community of hope and renewal you need to engage in the creation of great value.

God has called us to be certain kinds of people. We are people of assurance, of integrity, and of authenticity. When, by God's grace, these virtues flow from us as God-given gifts, they send us out into the workplace as expressions of the loving and redeeming presence of God.

God has called us to do certain kinds of work. He has called us to work that promotes personal well-being, promotes community well-being, and proceeds from and is an expression of Christian compassion. When our work is guided and sanctified by Christ's love, we make "sacred and social" that which our fallen cultures all too often make "secular and individual."

Let me leave you with the example of an everyday businessman, an extraordinary man to be sure, a man called by God to do his work in the spirit of the Wesleyan heritage that has shaped his faith. Meet Tom Collins.

A Leader Who Cares

Tom Collins is the president of a business known for its family tradition of excellence. Founded in 1980 by his father and uncle, CVS Systems, Inc., was built on values and principles such as keeping your word, being consistent with customers, and being honest.

The company is a DISH Network distributor for retailers in seven states. "We sell to people who sell to the public. We work hard to serve our customers and help them to achieve the results they want to achieve," Tom said. "Our competitors may sell for less money, and when we sell for more yet have more business, they're befuddled. But we know if we work hard for them, loyalty will follow."

These principles have rolled into the way Tom provides leadership to company employees. "We meet with our employees on a consistent basis, one or two times a month. These meetings focus the company's progress, things to improve on, anniversaries, and the like," he explained. But for about four years now, Tom has been showing concern for employees at a much deeper level. With their permission, he has been sharing employees' personal concerns with the group at large. This results in people encouraging others with a pat on the back, sending positive notes, and even offering to pray for each other.

Tom noted, "It is wonderful to see other people come behind them with compassion and changed attitudes. It creates a better work environment, and people know they and their families are valued . . . People spend more time at work than they spend with their families. It's hard to go to a place that doesn't care and park your problems at the door and go about your work. They thrive on knowing others care about them . . . We just want to see how we can love them better."

Caring can be contagious. "As I've started to watch people transform their behavior, things [problems] between them and other people have begun to vanish. I've seen people move to make differences in their lives," he observed. "As Christians, we're called to a higher calling, to help where God has called us to help. This is a way to tell the employees 'we're thinking about you,' 'praying about you'—a real way of applying faith in the workplace. It has been interesting to watch this develop, because now I'm getting requests on the second, third, fourth level out [concerns for the community]."

In addition, the circle of care has been developing in relationships with retailers, which was not intended in the beginning but has a life of its own, Tom declared. The company has an established fund to help people in the community who are in need. He said contributions come from a complete cross section of the employees, even those who are struggling themselves. "We look for those who are really struggling, and sometimes the money is going back to our own people and they don't even know it."

Tom stated, "I don't think anybody can argue with just caring for people. The proof is in the pudding, we have many long-term employees. They believe we care for them and are willing to stay, even though they might make more elsewhere. It's not about the money."

> Love impels one to do all possible good, of every possible kind, to all people . . .
>
> John Wesley

Bibliography

Acemoglu, Daron, and James A. Robinson. *Why Nations Fail: The Origins of Power, Prosperity and Poverty.* New York: Crown Business, Random House, 2012.

Clapper, Gregory S. *As If the Heart Mattered: A Wesleyan Spirituality.* Nashville: Upper Room Books, 1997.

Collins, Tom (President, CVS Systems, Inc.). In discussion with Rebecca Whitesel, June 2012.

Cornish Mining World Heritage Site. "Religion." http://www.cornish -mining.org.uk/delving-deeper/religion.

Covey, Stephen M. R., with Rebecca R. Merrill. *The Speed of Trust: The One Thing That Changes Everything.* New York: Free Press, 2006.

Dayton, Donald W. *Discovering an Evangelical Heritage.* Peabody, MA: Hendrickson, 1988. Originally published, New York: Harper & Row, 1976.

Edin, Kathryn, and Laura Lein. *Making Ends Meet: How Single Mothers Survive Welfare and Low-Wage Work.* New York: Russell Sage Foundation, 1997.

Foley, Chris (senior pastor, Grace Community Church, Maryborough, Queensland, Australia). In discussion with Rebecca Whitesel, June 2012.

Hamilton, Adam. *Enough: Discovering Joy through Simplicity and Generosity.* Nashville: Abingdon, 2009.

Harrison, W. H. "Loving the Creation, Loving the Creator: Dorothy L. Sayers's Theology of Work." *Anglican Theological Review* 86, pt. 2 (2004): 239–58.

Heitzenrater, Richard P. *Wesley and the People Called Methodists.* Nashville: Abingdon, 1995.

Hodges, Ralph (founder, Management Decisions Development Corp.). In discussion with Rebecca Whitesel, March 2012.

Jennings, Theodore W., Jr. *Good News to the Poor: John Wesley's Evangelical Economics.* Nashville: Abingdon, 1990.

Jenny. In discussion with Rebecca Whitesel, March 2012.

Jetter, George and Esther (founders, Fort Recovery Industries, Inc.). In discussion with Rebecca Whitesel, March 2012.

John Paul, Pope, II. *On Human Work: Encyclical Laborem Exercens.* Washington, DC: Office of Publishing Services, United States Catholic Conference, 1981. http://www.vatican.va/holy_father/john_paul_ii/encyclicals /documents/hf_jp-ii_enc_14091981_laborem-exercens_en.html.

Kelloway, E. Kevin, and Arla L. Day. "Building Healthy Workplaces: What We Know So Far." *Canadian Journal of Behavioural Science/Revue canadienne des sciences du comportement* 37, no. 4 (2005): 223–35. doi: 10.1037/h0087259. Also, http://ohpsychology.ca/wp-content /uploads/2011/02/day-kelloway-1.pdf.

Kingdon, Robert M. "Laissez-Faire or Government Control: A Problem for John Wesley." *Church History* 26, no. 4 (1957): 342–54.

Kirby, Katei. "Where Do You Go from Here?" *Christianity.* September 2010, 40–46. http://www.christianitymagazine.co.uk/Browse%20By%20 Category/features/Wheredoyougofromhere.aspx.

Kirby, Katei (ordained minister, trustee, and executive officer for international board, Wesleyan Holiness Church in the UK). In discussion with Christin Taylor, 2012.

LaBier, Douglas. "The Lowdown on Abusive Bosses and the Unhealthy Workplace—Part 1." *Psychology Today*, June 25, 2011. http:// www.psychologytoday.com/blog/the-new-resilience/201106/the -lowdown-abusive-bosses-and-the-unhealthy-workplace-part-1. For more on the referenced 2011 poll, see the Psychologically Healthy Workplace Program website, http://www.phwa.org/.

Levitin, Daniel. *This Is Your Brain on Music: The Science of a Human Obsession.* New York: Penguin, 2006.

Maddox, Randy. "The Holistic Vision of John Wesley: Q&A with Randy Maddox Part I." Interview by John Shorb. *Church Health Reader*, October 25, 2010. http://chreader.org/contentPage.aspx?resource _id=580.

Maddox, Randy L. *Responsible Grace: John Wesley's Practical Theology*. Nashville: Kingswood Books, 1994.

———. "'Visit the Poor': John Wesley, the Poor, and the Sanctification of Believers." In Richard P. Heitzenrater, ed. *The Poor and the People Called Methodists, 1729–1999*. Nashville: Kingswood Books, 2002. Proceedings of an international conference on "The Wesleys and the Poor: The Legacy and Development of Methodist Attitudes toward Poverty, 1739–1999" held at Bridwell Library in October 1999 at Southern Methodist University, University Park, Texas.

Methodist Church of Great Britain. *The Book of Offices: Being the Orders of Service Authorized for Use in the Methodist Church Together with the Order of Morning Prayer*. London: Methodist Publishing House, 1936.

NgTrader. "The History of Boots the Chemist—Nottingham," http:// ngtrader.co.uk/thebootsstory.htm. Also see Books UK, Alliance Boots. "Boots History." http://www.boots-uk.com/About_Boots /Boots_Heritage/Boots_History.aspx.

Noll, Mark A. *The Rise of Evangelicalism: The Age of Edwards, Whitefield, and the Wesleys*. History of Evangelicalism 1. Downers Grove, IL: Inter-Varsity, 2003.

Outler, Albert C., ed. *John Wesley*. Library of Protestant Thought. New York: Oxford University Press, 1964.

Outler, Albert C., and Richard P. Heitzenrater, eds. *John Wesley's Sermons: An Anthology*. Nashville: Abingdon, 1991. Selected sermons originally published in *The Works of John Wesley*, vols. 1–4: Sermons I–IV. Nashville: Abingdon, 1984–87.

People Bottomline. http://www.thepeoplebottomline.com/. Formerly the Worktrauma.org website.

Phillippe, Tom, Sr., and Joan (former general director of evangelism for the Wesleyan Church; retired minister and businessman, Nationwide Care, Inc.). In discussion with Rebecca Whitesel, March 2012.

Runyon, Theodore. *The New Creation: John Wesley's Theology Today.* Nashville: Abingdon, 1998.

————. "The New Creation: A Wesleyan Distinctive." *Wesleyan Theological Journal* 31, no. 2 (1996): 5–19. http://wesley.nnu.edu/fileadmin /imported_site/wesleyjournal/1996-wtj-31-2.pdf.

Sauter, Steven L., Lawrence R. Murphy, and Joseph J. Hurrell. "Prevention of Work-Related Psychological Disorders: A National Strategy Proposed by the National Institute for Occupational Safety and Health (NIOSH)." *American Psychologist* 45, no. 10 (1990): 1146–58. doi: 10.1037/0003-066X.45.10.1146.

Sayers, Dorothy L. "Why Work?" In *Creed or Chaos? And Other Essays in Popular Theology.* London: Methuen, 1947. Published in the United States, New York: Harcourt, Brace, 1949. Reprint, Manchester, NH: Sophia Institute Press, 1995.

Schofield, Robert E. "John Wesley and Science in 18th Century England." *Isis* 44, no. 4 (1953): 331–40.

Simon, Herbert, and Kevin J. Gilmartin. "A Simulation of Memory for Chess Positions." *Cognitive Psychology* 5 (1973): 29–46. http:// www.cs.wright.edu/~snarayan/isis/pdf/group5one.pdf.

Sloane, Ken (director of stewardship for the General Board of Discipleship, The United Methodist Church). In discussion with Rebecca Whitesel, March 2012.

Snyder, Dean. "Social Holiness: Our Wesleyan DNA," Jeremiah 8:18–22 (sermon, Foundry United Methodist Church, Washington, DC, October 5, 2003). Written version available at http://www.foundryumc .org/sermons/10_5_2003.pdf.

Stanton, Keith (director, BAPM New Zealand Ltd.; trust administrator; commercial property manager). In discussion with Rebecca Whitesel, March 2012.

Thorsen, Don. *The Wesleyan Quadrilateral: Scripture, Tradition, Reason, and Experience as a Model for Evangelical Theology.* Lexington: Emeth Press, 2005. Reprint, 1990.

Turnbull, Colin M. *The Human Cycle.* New York: Simon and Schuster, 1983.

Wesley, John. *The Character of a Methodist* (tract, n.p., 1742). In *The Works of John Wesley*. Edited by Thomas Jackson. 14 vols. London, Wesleyan Conference Office, 1872. Earlier reprint, New York: Waugh and Mason, 1835. Preface date, 1831. New York, NY: General Board of Global Ministries, 2012. http://www.umcmission.org/Find-Resources/Global-Worship-and-Spiritual-Growth/The-Wesleys-and-Their-Times/The-Character-of-a-Methodist.

———. "Heaviness through Manifold Temptations." 1 Peter 1:6 (sermon, n.p., n.d.). In *Sermons of John Wesley, 1872 Edition*. Edited by Thomas Jackson. Wesley Center Online. Online text edited by Tim Dawson with corrections by Ryan Danker and George Lyons for the Wesley Center for Applied Theology at Northwest Nazarene University, Nampa, ID. http://wesley.nnu.edu/john-wesley/the-sermons-of-john-wesley-1872-edition/sermon-47-heaviness-through-manifold-temptations/. The text for John Wesley's sermons in all preceding and subsequent citations originally came from the Christian Classics Ethereal Library, www.ccel.org.

———. "The Image of God." Genesis 1:27 (sermon, n.p., 1730). In *John Wesley's Sermons: An Anthology*, edited by Albert C. Outler and Richard P. Heitzenrater, 14–21 (Nashville: Abingdon, 1991).

———. John Wesley to Miss March, 7 February 1776, London. In *The Letters of John Wesley*. Vol. 6. Edited by John Telford. London: Epworth Press, 1931. Wesley Center Online. Online text edited by George Lyons and Michael Mattei for the Wesley Center for Applied Theology at Northwest Nazarene University, Nampa, ID. http://wesley.nnu.edu/john-wesley/the-letters-of-john-wesley/wesleys-letters-1776/. Also quoted in Maddox, "'Visit the Poor'" cited above.

———. "The Law Established through Faith: Discourse Two." Romans 3:31 (sermon, n.p., 1750). In *Sermons of John Wesley, 1872 Edition*. Edited by Thomas Jackson. Wesley Center Online. Online text edited by Jennette Descalzo with corrections by Ryan Danker for the Wesley Center for Applied Theology at Northwest Nazarene University, Nampa, ID. http://wesley.nnu.edu/john-wesley/the-sermons-of-john-wesley-1872-edition/sermon-36-the-law-established-through-faith-discourse-two/.

———. "The More Excellent Way." 1 Corinthians 12:31 (sermon, n.p., 1787). In *Sermons of John Wesley, 1872 Edition*. Edited by Thomas Jackson. Wesley Center Online. Online text edited by Edward Purkey with corrections by Ryan Danker and George Lyons for the Wesley Center for Applied Theology at Northwest Nazarene University, Nampa, ID. http://wesley.nnu.edu/john-wesley/the-sermons-of -john-wesley-1872-edition/sermon-89-the-more-excellent-way/.

———. "The Nature, Design, and General Rules of the United Societies (1743)." In *The Methodist Societies: History, Nature, and Design*. Edited by Rupert E. Davis. Vol. 9 of *The Bicentennial Edition of the Works of John Wesley*, 68–73. Nashville: Abingdon, 1989.

———. "On Charity." 1 Corinthians 13:1–3 (sermon, n.p., n.d.). In *Sermons of John Wesley, 1872 Edition*. Edited by Thomas Jackson. Wesley Center Online. Online text edited by Kevin Farrow with corrections by Ryan Danker and George Lyons for the Wesley Center for Applied Theology at Northwest Nazarene University, Nampa, ID. http://wesley.nnu.edu/john-wesley/the-sermons-of-john-wesley -1872-edition/sermon-91-on-charity/.

———. "The One Thing Needful." Luke 10:42 (sermon, St. Mary's, Oxford, England; Boston, New England; London, England, et al., 1734–38). In *John Wesley's Sermons: An Anthology*, edited by Albert C. Outler and Richard P. Heitzenrater, 34–38 (Nashville: Abingdon, 1991).

———. "Preface." In John Wesley and Charles Wesley. *Hymns and Sacred Poems*. London: W. Strahan, 1739. Vol. 14 of *The Works of John Wesley*. Edited by Thomas Jackson. London: Wesleyan-Methodist Book Room, 1872.

———. *Primitive Physick: or, An Easy and Natural Method of Curing Most Diseases*. London: G. Woodfall, 1747. http://www.umcmission.org /Find-Resources/Global-Worship-and-Spiritual-Growth/The-Wesleys -and-Their-Times/Primitive-Physick. Wesley first published his book anonymously in 1747 (2nd ed.). Not until 1760 (8th ed.) did he place his name on it.

———. "The Scripture Way of Salvation." Ephesians 2:8 (sermon, n.p., 1765). In *Sermons of John Wesley, 1872 Edition*. Edited by Thomas Jackson. Wesley Center Online. Online text edited by Anne-

Elizabeth Powell with minor corrections and formatting by Ryan Danker and George Lyons for the Wesley Center for Applied Theology at Northwest Nazarene University, Nampa, ID. http://wesley.nnu.edu/john-wesley/the-sermons-of-john-wesley-1872-edition/sermon-43-the-scripture-way-of-salvation/.

———. "Upon Our Lord's Sermon on the Mount: Discourse Three." Matthew 5:8–12 (sermon, n.p., n.d.). In *Sermons of John Wesley, 1872 Edition*. Edited by Thomas Jackson. Wesley Center Online. Online text edited by Jennette Descalzo with corrections by Ryan Danker and George Lyons for the Wesley Center for Applied Theology at Northwest Nazarene University, Nampa, ID. http://wesley.nnu.edu/john-wesley/the-sermons-of-john-wesley-1872-edition/sermon-23-upon-our-lords-sermon-on-the-mount-discourse-three/.

———. "The Use of Money." Luke 16:9 (sermon, n.p., n.d.). In *Sermons of John Wesley, 1872 Edition*. Edited by Thomas Jackson. Wesley Center Online. Online text edited by Jennette Descalzo with corrections by George Lyons and further formatting by Ryan Danker for the Wesley Center for Applied Theology at Northwest Nazarene University, Nampa, ID. http://wesley.nnu.edu/john-wesley/the-sermons-of-john-wesley-1872-edition/sermon-50-the-use-of-money/.

Williams, Wilbur (associate professor of biblical literature and archaeology, Indiana Wesleyan University). In discussion with Rebecca Whitesel, April 2012.

Wilson, William J. *When Work Disappears: The World of the New Urban Poor.* New York: Knopf, 1996. Vintage Books edition distributed by Random House.

Workplace Bullying Institute. "Who Gets Targeted." June 22, 2011. http://www.workplacebullying.org/individuals/problem/who-gets-targeted/.

Workplace Bullying Institute, and Gary Namie. *2010 WBI U.S. Workplace Bullying Survey.* Conducted by Zogby International. Bellingham, WA, Workplace Bullying Institute, 2010. http://www.workplacebullying.org/wbiresearch/2010-wbi-national-survey/.

Yrigoyen, Charles, Jr. *John Wesley: Holiness of Heart and Life.* Nashville: Abingdon, 1996. See especially chapters 1–3.

About the Contributors

David Wright (PhD, University of Kentucky) serves as provost and chief academic officer at Indiana Wesleyan University. He has a strong interest in international higher education having held positions in Haiti and England in addition to his work in the United States. Dr. Wright is the author of Finding Freedom from Fear: A Contemporary Study from the Psalms and Wisdom as a Lifestyle: Building Biblical Life-Codes. He is also an ordained minister in the Wesleyan Church.

Rebecca Whitesel (BA, Purdue University) serves as an award-winning journalist, editor, and publicist who specializes in public relations and human interest stories. She is the editor of *House & Home*, a home resource magazine serving the Michiana region.

Christin Taylor (MFA, Antioch University Los Angeles) serves as an adjunct assistant professor of English at Gettysburg College and also teaches writing through her own Blank Page Writing Workshops. She is currently awaiting publication of her first book, *Shipwrecked in Los Angeles* (2013), and is working on her second book. Christin and her husband, Dwayne, and their daughter, Noelle, live in Gettysburg, Pennsylvania.

Patrick Eby (PhD cand., Drew University) serves as an adjunct professor of church history for Indiana Wesleyan University and Asbury Theological Seminary. His study has focused on the history and theology of the early Methodist movement.

He is currently working on his first book, *The Heart of Charles Wesley's Theology: Being Restored in the Image of God.*

Keith Reeves (PhD, Union Theological Seminary) serves as a professor of New Testament and early Christian literature at Azusa Pacific University and is an ordained minister in the Wesleyan Church. He also holds an MBA and is involved in a number of business ventures. He and his wife, Karen, reside in La Verne, California, and have three daughters.